This book is due for return on or before the last date shown below.

Student Helpbook Series

Lifetime Careers

Careers with an Arts or Humanities Degree – fourth edition
Published by Lifetime Publishing, Mill House, Stallard Street,
Trowbridge BA14 8HH

© Nord Anglia Lifetime Development South West Ltd, 2006

ISBN 1 904979 06 8

ISBN-13 978 1904979 06 7

Printed and bound by Cromwell Press Ltd, Trowbridge
Cover design by Lesley May
Illustrations by Joe Wright

Contents

About the author

Philip Schofield is a freelance writer specialising in careers and employment. He has been research director of a major recruitment advertising agency, marketing director of one careers publishing house, and research and editorial director of another. Much of his research work has been on the factors affecting career choice – especially of graduates.

He has been a consultant to many leading employers, employment bureaux, recruitment advertising agencies and the media. He has also researched and written graduate recruitment literature for more than 30 major employers.

Philip has lectured internationally, and was a founder member and the first secretary of the Manpower Society, on the Committee of the Recruitment Society, edited the journals *Personnel Executive* and *International Recruitment World*, and is a member of the Careers Writers Association. He has written regularly on higher education for *The Independent* and on careers for *The Independent on Sunday, The Daily Telegraph, The Times, The Sunday Times* and for many magazines. He has co-authored three books on recruitment and contributed to a wide range of careers literature.

Acknowledgements

I would like to thank the many professional institutions, government departments and agencies, employers, publishers, learned societies and universities who have helped me with information and advice. I am particularly grateful to the Association of Graduate Recruiters, High Flyers Research and the Institute for Employment Studies.

Thanks also to the graduates who were prepared to tell their stories for inclusion as profiles in this edition: Jake Eliot, Matthew Styant, Jennie Hood, Rebecca Swainson, Nathan Webb and Charlene McManus.

Finally, I wish to express my lifelong appreciation to my wife Irene. Without her love and constant support I could never have undertaken a portfolio career or become a full-time writer. To her I offer my love and gratitude.

Philip Schofield

How to use this book

Whether you are thinking of studying for an arts or humanities degree, are already doing so, or have recently graduated, this book is for you.

As you probably know, arts and humanities degrees are sometimes seen as having limited vocational value. This book aims to dispel that myth and to describe the huge range of career opportunities open to you.

The first section of this book looks at the value of studying these subjects, and particularly at how employers rate them. It then offers advice on choosing a degree course (Chapter two). Because the ways in which people work are changing faster than ever before, Chapter three discusses the trends affecting the employment of arts and humanities graduates. Finally, because employers of graduates are not just interested in academic qualifications but also in what you can do, Chapter four describes the key skills that you should try to develop before starting your job search.

Section 2 looks at careers that could make direct use of your degree subject, while Section 3 looks at careers outside your degree subject which would still be open to you. In summarising each career, the aim is to describe the nature of the work, 'warts and all', and to give you an indication of the training you'll undertake, the opportunities it offers for career progression, any personal qualities you'll need and some major sources of job vacancy information. Around two-thirds of graduate vacancies are now open to graduates of any discipline, so you have a wide choice of career areas open to you. In fact, a number of the jobs described in Section 2, which link directly to a particular degree subject, are also open to graduates of other disciplines, so don't overlook these career areas too!

It is impossible in one book to provide a full description of every career open to arts and humanities graduates. The aim here is to give enough information for you to decide which careers you want to investigate further. Section 4 details some sources of additional advice and information.

Because 'arts and humanities' cover such a wide range of subjects, you will find a brief description of the main disciplines on the next three pages.

Please note: The term 'university' is used throughout this book as shorthand for 'university or college/institute of higher education'.

What subjects are covered by arts and humanities?

Arts subjects are sometimes called 'the humanities', although this originally meant the study of Greek and Latin. The range of arts and humanities subjects is very wide and can be confusing because similar names are used to describe courses that are very different from one another.

The following list summarises the main subject areas and outlines the range of topics within them.

Archaeology: This is the study of the non-documentary remains of the past. There is a significant science component because of the techniques now used for the identification, dating and preservation of archaeological finds. Some courses specialise in classical (Greek and Roman) archaeology, others in conservation or the science of archaeology.

Area studies: Often linked with modern language studies, these cover the geography, economics, politics, and other aspects of contemporary society and culture of a particular country or area.

Art and design: Normally a single subject is studied, possibly with a specialist topic within it. Subjects range from three-dimensional design (such as ceramics or furniture) to scientific illustration, fine art and photographic studies.

Art history: Courses may be general or specialist. They deal with the history of painting, sculpture, architecture, fashion, furniture, film and photography, and cover periods ranging from antiquity to the present time.

Classics: This covers the study of the history, philosophy, literature and art of the ancient world. Some, but not all, courses include studying Greek or Latin, or both.

Communication and media studies: Typical course titles include media, culture and society; psychology, communication and computing; film, video and photographic arts; public relations; and journalism and social science. Most of these are not vocational courses leading to careers in 'the media'. Rather, they deal with issues relating to the role of media in society.

Dance, drama and performing arts: Degree studies combine theory and practice, although the balance between the two varies. Most drama courses are weighted to the historical, social and literary aspects of theatre. Dance and performing arts studies are more concerned with the practical aspects of the subjects.

English: Most courses are concerned with literature rather than language, but some balance the two. Courses include options to specialise, for example in 19th-century literature or creative writing.

Fashion and textiles: These are design courses and can range from studying textiles or fashion, alone or in combination, through to courses that include shoe, knitwear and lingerie design. Many courses include the business side of the industry, and some offer a language option.

History: Studies in history may be categorised by period (ancient, medieval or modern), by type (for example political, economic or social) and by place (American, English, East Mediterranean, Scottish, etc). There is an almost infinite range of options.

Linguistics: This is the scientific study of language. It is concerned with the structure and sounds of languages and with how and why languages evolve. Most courses offer specialist options.

Modern languages: Some courses emphasise studying the literature of a language or country, while others concentrate on developing practical skills. Most degrees cover two languages, and studying a third is sometimes an option. Languages are also a component of many courses in area studies.

Music: University courses combine academic study with music-making in differing proportions. There is enormous variety in the types of music studied – from Western classical to the music of the Far East, from electronic to pop. Colleges of music also offer degree courses that are more vocationally orientated and so concentrate on performance, conducting or composing.

Philosophy: This is the study of ideas, the discipline of thought, the nature of argument and the search for ultimate truths. It includes the study of logic, ethics (moral philosophy) and metaphysics. There is usually a range of options.

Theology: This covers the study of religious doctrines. In Western Europe these are usually of the Judaeo-Christian tradition. There are also specialist courses, including Jewish studies. Other courses (usually called religious studies or comparative religion) cover a range of world religions.

Most of these subjects can be studied in combination with others. You will find more about this in Chapter two.

Section I

Why study arts
or humanities?

Chapter one
The value of studying arts or humanities

We read and hear a lot about the vocational importance of a university education. So you may well wonder why more than one in three students today still choose to take a non-vocational degree in the arts or humanities. In fact, there are two excellent reasons for taking them: firstly because you are really interested in an arts or humanities subject for its own sake, and secondly because much of the graduate job market is open to graduates in these subjects. However, you'll find that people do have mixed views on their value.

'All art is quite useless.'

Oscar Wilde, playwright, novelist and poet

'Art is the expression of the profoundest thoughts in the simplest way.'

Albert Einstein, scientist

In recent years there has been a lot of emphasis on how education should prepare you for the world of work. This has led some people to believe that arts and humanities subjects are much less useful than, say, science, technology or business studies. They think that a university education should prepare you for a specific type of job, and nothing more. They expect you to make a firm choice of career and then select the most appropriate degree course to qualify you for that career. This ignores the fact that most young people quite understandably don't know what they eventually want to do at this early stage. Moreover, most graduate employers are far less interested in the specific knowledge you get from your degree course than in the skills it teaches you and the personal qualities that you develop. And many of the skills learned on arts and humanities courses are very much in demand from employers. Let's ask some basic questions and look at the facts.

Should you choose a degree course for vocational reasons?

Only a minority of vacancies for graduates specify a particular subject. Around two-thirds of graduate vacancies are now open to those with a degree in any discipline, including the arts and humanities subjects. However, some careers require a specific degree. If you're really sure that you want to enter a 'closed' profession like medicine or architecture, then it is essential that you study for a relevant vocational degree. You cannot enter these careers without an appropriate degree. There are many more careers for which you can choose to take a relevant degree – such as teaching, management, journalism and accountancy – but it isn't essential. Oddly, some professional institutions find that those with a relevant degree often do less well than those with a non-relevant degree. The Institute for Employment Studies has pointed out that, even in vocational areas such as accountancy and law, many employers recruit, and indeed often prefer, graduates who have studied unrelated subjects. Obviously, these employers must then provide the necessary job-specific training and career development. If you later think you might benefit from a vocational qualification, you could consider taking a relevant postgraduate course after a non-relevant degree.

If you have no idea what you'd like to do and so choose your degree because you enjoy the subject, you won't be alone. Surveys carried out in the past show that only one in five students choose their degree course for vocational reasons. Most choose a subject that interests them. Most young people don't know what career they want to follow until they are near the end of their university education, and not always then. This is hardly surprising.

By the time you complete your degree you will be a different person with different aspirations. You will be more mature, more confident of your strengths and have a better understanding of your weaknesses. You will have discovered new interests and developed a more detailed knowledge of the opportunities open to you. Moreover, the world will have moved on and there will have been significant changes in the graduate employment market.

Unless you're absolutely certain that you want to follow a particular career, defer any decision until you're in your second year at university. By then, you'll know a lot more about yourself and about the openings available, and you'll still have plenty of time to prepare for your job search. You don't have to choose a career in order to select a degree course and, in fact, you might be wise not to do so.

Is an arts or humanities degree an easy option?

Many arts and humanities courses are both intellectually rigorous and hard to get accepted onto, because of their popularity. As the number of places is limited, it can be harder to get onto these courses than many in the sciences. And because of the level of competition for places you will, on average, need better qualifications than you would to enter a science course.

There are many arts and humanities subjects – including classics, history, modern languages and philosophy – that normally require you to work at least as hard as you would in any other area. The intellectual rigour of many of these courses is respected both by the academic world and by graduate employers. On the other hand, there are some arts and humanities courses that are easier options. You can usually identify these by the fewer points required by the Universities and Colleges Admissions Service (UCAS) for entry to these courses. However, some good courses that are undersubscribed may have lower entry requirements, so you need to choose carefully.

But if you have the ability to get good UCAS points and are career minded, you are best aiming for a less easy course requiring a good level of UCAS points. Easy options seldom impress graduate employers. A growing number of graduate recruiters today not only specify the class of degree you have earned, but also the minimum number of UCAS points they expect you to have.

Do employers value arts and humanities degrees?

Few employers specify arts or humanities subjects for their graduate vacancies (although there are exceptions – such as in art and design, specialist teaching and foreign languages). Graduates with a science/technology degree do have some advantage over arts and humanities graduates in the job market. They tend to find a job more easily and have a higher starting salary. However, the differences are not so great that they should be major considerations in choosing a degree subject. Numerous surveys over the years show that most graduates are less concerned with a good salary than with personal and professional fulfilment. For instance, the 2004 survey of 3,800 UK students by the Swedish consultancy Universum Communications found that only 11% 'are influenced by competitive rates of pay and benefits' when describing attractive employer qualities. Among the 11 factors rated more highly were, in order of importance: international career opportunities; flexible working hours; variety of assignments; secure employment; a formal graduate training programme; and increasing challenging tasks.

In filling vacancies, most employers prefer intellectually rigorous disciplines. These are not just science and technology subjects, but also include such arts and humanities disciplines as classics, linguistics, history and philosophy.

Any degree course combines subject knowledge with skills that have almost universal application. These are called 'key skills' by the Government. Outside science and technology, most employers are concerned less with the knowledge content of your degree than they are with the key skills you've acquired. (Key skills are discussed more fully in Chapter four.) Among the key skills you should acquire (in order of importance to graduate recruiters) are:

- interpersonal skills

- team working

- oral communication

- problem solving

- managing your own development

- written communication

- time management

- business awareness

- numeracy (application of number)

- information technology/computer literacy.

Each skill is important to employers. However, many complain that graduates in disciplines outside the arts and humanities have poor communication and interpersonal skills, and so have difficulty in presenting arguments clearly and logically and in working with colleagues. These graduates may have a wealth of technical knowledge, but often they can explain it only to other technical specialists.

As you will see in Chapter three, the ways in which employers use graduates are changing dramatically. Employers are putting even greater emphasis on key skills, and especially on the ability to communicate well. Many of these changes are likely to favour arts and humanities graduates. In careers where communication skills are particularly important, the arts or humanities graduate has a distinct advantage. These careers are not just the obvious ones like publishing, advertising, journalism and sales. Good communication skills are also vital in such careers as banking, accountancy, business management, the Civil Service, local government and the Armed Forces.

Each year, the Association of Graduate Recruiters (AGR), whose members collectively recruit around 30,000 graduates a year, publishes an annual survey of the vacancies and salaries offered by its members. The 2005 study found that 17% of AGR employers reported that they anticipated difficulty filling their graduate vacancies. Many (44%) said that this is because there are 'not enough applicants with the suitable skills – namely leadership, communication and other business skills'.

These skills are especially important to employers who look for high potential entrants to their management training schemes.

'Generally, employers seek graduates with leadership potential and the selection criteria focus on a cluster of competencies seen as critical to leadership:

- intellectual ability, linked to analytical skills and strategic thinking

- interpersonal skills, seen as linked both to influencing skills and to the future ability to manage and motivate staff

- drive to achieve results, seen as linked to personal effectiveness.'

'Fishing for talent in a wider pool: trends and dilemmas in corporate graduate recruitment', Institute for Employment Studies, September 2005

Will you be trapped by your degree subject?

Many final year undergraduates feel trapped by their subject. Some worry that their career choice will be restricted by the specialist nature of their degree subject. Others, studying subjects in which they've lost interest, worry that they will be trapped in a career related to their course.

Surveys suggest that one in four undergraduates would, if given their time over again, have chosen a different course. If you feel that this might happen to you, don't worry. Your choice of degree subject won't limit you to a career in that discipline. Very many graduates enter careers that have nothing to do with their degree subject. The fact that lots of graduates end up in jobs unrelated to their subject doesn't mean their studies have been wasted. The intellectual and practical skills and experience that you acquire at university are often of most importance to employers. Remember that most graduate jobs are open to all disciplines.

'As a scientist myself, I feel it is of especial importance to emphasise the importance and value of humanities to a university... The humanities are, in a sense, the custodians of our culture. The study of them provides profound intellectual satisfaction and pleasure; it provides the fundamentals of ethics and the processes by which we communicate ideas and comprehend languages; and they provide understanding of beauty whether it is perceived by the written word, by music or by the visual senses. The humanities truly provide an excellent education.'

Sir David Smith, former Principal of the University of Edinburgh

Key points to think about

You might like to discuss these points with your parents, a guardian or friends.

- Most students don't choose a career until near graduation.

- Only one in five students chooses their degree course for vocational reasons.

- Most students worry about being typecast by their discipline.

- Most students gain new interests and discover new horizons during their studies.

- Some vocational degrees limit career options more than those that are non-vocational.

- Many arts and humanities courses are highly respected for their intellectual rigour.

- Arts and humanities courses provide key skills essential to most employers.

- Most graduate job vacancies are open to arts and humanities graduates.

Chapter two
Why choose arts or humanities?

'There is no such thing on earth as an uninteresting subject; the only thing that can exist is an uninteresting person.'

G K Chesterton, British writer

Obviously, you want to make the right decisions about your degree course. Your family, naturally, is anxious that you do so. Others too, including your teachers, friends and relatives, want to see you on the right path. You're not likely to be short of advice. Whatever advice you're given – good, bad or indifferent – it's you and nobody else who must make the final decision. You're the one who'll have to live with the consequences, not only at university, but throughout your working life.

There are several things to think about when choosing a degree subject and then a particular university or college course. These include your personal interests and aptitudes; career prospects; your subjects and grades at GCSE or Standard grades – and more especially AS/A levels and Highers/Advanced Highers or their equivalents; the types of course available; where you would like to study; and teaching standards.

Personal interests

The best reason for choosing a particular degree course is that you find the subject completely fascinating and that it is something you really want to do. Not only will this give you intellectual satisfaction, but your interest in the subject will help you to stay motivated throughout your studies.

You may have already done one of the computer or paper-and-pencil tests available to examine your interests and current aptitudes. If so, you were probably given a list of jobs compatible with your self-description. Treat this list with some caution; the tests can't probe your answers. There are three reasons to be cautious:

- your interest in a subject (or rejection of other subjects) could be based on false assumptions

- your school experiences are not a reliable guide to what a particular subject will be like at university or college

- universities offer a marvellous range of courses in fascinating subjects that you've probably never met at school.

Aptitudes

You need to consider your existing aptitudes – what you're currently good at. Most of us are better at subjects we like than at those we dislike, but not always. On the other hand, don't underestimate your aptitudes. Don't assume that what you've done to date is all you can do, or what you could be best at. Most of us also discover new aptitudes and interests while we are in higher education.

Your aptitudes may have also been assessed through tests. If not, there are three ways you could do this: through your school; through a book of self-assessment tests; or through a qualified occupational psychologist. There are more details about how assessment might help you and about other sources of advice in Section 4 of this book.

A few years ago, in a series of major annual surveys of final-year students, MORI asked how they would describe themselves. They found that arts students were more likely than others to describe themselves as somebody who:

■ likes working with people

■ is hard working

■ is imaginative

■ has a broad outlook on life.

On the other hand, they were less likely than others to describe themselves as somebody who:

■ has an analytical mind

■ is practical

■ is very ambitious

■ is motivated by money

■ has a technical mind.

It might help to think about how these descriptions relate to you.

Career prospects

Many people, including some parents, believe that the purpose of a degree course is to train students for work related to the course subject, but this is misleading. A degree prepares one for life, not just work. Moreover, most graduates are recruited for their trained minds rather than their specialist knowledge. They know how to learn systematically, how to handle and interpret information, and how to analyse and solve problems. Employers also value the maturity, social skills and self-confidence that can come from three or more years of university life. So, for most people, the value of studying for a degree is that it allows them to pursue an interest in a particular subject while developing intellectual skills that are valued by employers.

'Every arts graduate learns to challenge premises and to question processes. The arts graduate is not simply trained in flexibility, but is educated in intelligence. Can there be any better preparation for the brave new world of the next millennium?'

Professor Michael Wharton of University College London, cited in Careerscope

Nevertheless, bear in mind when choosing your subject that not all arts or humanities subjects are given equal weight by employers. Because they seek 'trained minds', most employers prefer graduates who've read a subject with a reputation for intellectual rigour. Arts and humanities subjects such as archaeology, classics, history, linguistics, philosophy and theology have a higher reputation for rigour among employers than many vocational courses or such social science subjects as sociology, politics and education. On the other hand, you should be cautious when choosing 'modular' courses, even in rigorous subjects. Modules make possible some interesting combinations of topics, but some employers (and academics too) are worried that badly selected modularised degrees may only allow superficial coverage of a discipline. Employers are more impressed by the in-depth study of one subject than they are by a shallow dabbling in many. Make sure the combination of modules you choose is a useful one that you can justify to employers.

The best approach is to choose a subject in which you have a passionate interest, but to be aware of employer attitudes to that subject. Let's look at two examples.

Language skills

British employers are very short of foreign language skills. According to a 2002 study by Hobsons only one in three UK graduates is confident enough to go abroad to work, compared to the two-thirds of their counterparts in other European countries. A British Chambers of

Commerce survey in 2004 found that 80% of export managers cannot do business in even one foreign language. Another survey, the 2004 International Business Owners survey by accountants Grant Thornton, found that the proportion of UK executives who could negotiate in more than one language was half the EU average and well below the global average. And in 2005 a Korn/Ferry International survey of recruiters found that nine in ten executive recruiters believe that the ability to speak another language is 'critical to success' in Europe, Asia/Pacific and Latin America.

As you can see, there are good opportunities to use modern language within business. However, very few people are hired solely for their language skills. Consequently, it is wise to combine a foreign language with another subject. Most posts that specifically demand a language-only degree are in translation, interpretation and teaching English as a foreign language. You need to consider whether you would find these jobs satisfying in the long term.

Overseas employers, similarly, expect a vocational subject combined with one or more modern languages. British universities offer a good range of suitable courses. Among the many vocational subjects you can combine with foreign languages are accountancy, marketing, journalism, law, business and management.

Art, performing arts and design

Employers outside the relevant areas see courses in art, design, music, drama and dance as less rigorous than other subjects. But to employers in related fields these courses may be essential qualifications. If any of these subjects interest you, you should be aware of two facts.

Firstly, unemployment among newly qualified art and design graduates is significantly higher than for most other disciplines. Secondly, there are even fewer vacancies in careers directly related to music, drama and dance, and most of these require further postgraduate study. This isn't meant to discourage you from following one of these subjects if you've a passionate interest in it and the necessary talent. But do be prepared for a very competitive job market and further study.

Your subjects and grades

The subjects you've taken at school will give you an idea of the areas of study that interest you, and your grades will tell you whether you've got an aptitude for them. However, don't overlook your recreational activities because these may be an even better guide to your underlying interests. Your choice of degree subject and course will be limited by your examination results at both A level and GCSE (or their equivalents). For example, if you want to study history, not only is an A level in history required for some degree courses, but so too is a language at GCSE (grades A*-C).

The courses available

You face a bewildering choice. There are over 900 degree subjects and more than 55,000 courses covering every conceivable discipline. The range is even larger than you might guess from looking through lists of courses, because degrees at different universities may have the same name but their content can differ a lot.

All UK courses are listed in the annual *University and College Entrance: The Official Guide*. This is often called the 'Big Guide' and is published by the Universities and Colleges Admissions Service (UCAS). You should find a copy in the careers library of your secondary school or in any good public reference library. This comes with a CD-ROM containing all the entry requirements. You can also search courses through the UCAS website: www.ucas.com

You could also consult resources such as the *Which Degree* series (published annually by Hobsons), especially volume 1 covering arts, humanities and languages. The series gives brief details of the content of every UK degree course. And see the *CRAC Degree Course Guides* in your chosen subjects, also published by Hobsons. You may find these at your careers/Connexions centre. Otherwise contact the publisher (addresses in Chapter twenty-two).

You may also be able to consult a course database in your school or college. The main one is *Course Discover* (supplied to schools on a subscription basis) by ECTIS and Trotman Information Services.

You can get more information on this by logging on to www.trotman. co.uk/coursediscover/

Once you have narrowed down your choice, study the undergraduate prospectuses to find out in detail exactly what each university is offering. More and more faculties and departments are also publishing their own handbooks, which give a more detailed picture of the course content, teaching methods, entrance requirements, academic staff and research interests. All institutions now have websites that are listed in the UCAS 'Big Guide'.

The traditional degree course covers one subject (a single honours degree). However, there is a wide choice of courses on which you can study two or more subjects. These are very popular. You could take a two-subject course (a joint honours degree), for example, combining modern languages with one of the following:

- accountancy
- archaeology
- business and management
- classical studies
- computer science
- economics
- film and TV studies
- geography
- history of art
- journalism
- law
- marketing
- mathematics
- modern history

- music
- philosophy
- physics
- politics
- religious studies
- theatre studies.

There are also combined honours courses that let you choose a number of modules from a seemingly infinite range of subjects. These have a variety of names, including combined studies, modular studies, cultural studies, independent study, general honours, general arts, and humanities.

You may also come across a few relevant 'foundation degree' courses. While primarily vocational courses, available foundation degrees include archaeology, applied art and design, history and heritage management, and English with history. Foundation degrees are two-year courses, full-time (and are also available on a part-time basis) designed to equip students with the skills employers need. It is usually possible to top-up to an honours degree through further study. (N.B. Don't confuse foundation degrees with the art foundation courses that lead onto art and design degrees.) For more details, see the UCAS website: www.ucas.com

Where to study?

Universities and colleges differ not only in the subjects they offer and the content of their courses, but also in how they teach and assess you. Read the prospectuses carefully. Teaching quality varies a lot – some courses have a better reputation with schools and with employers than others. Many employers target specific universities and courses for recruitment. *Where* you take your degree can now be very important in terms of your employability.

Growing numbers of young people now opt to study close to home to avoid getting into too much debt. This offers financial advantages during your time at university. However, a study of 13,000 graduates by two economists at Newcastle University has found that those who study away from home have better job prospects. It found that, of the students who moved away from home to study, 69.9% were prepared to move to work. This compared with 37.6% of those who studied locally. A willingness to move improves your job prospects. Moreover, those who have lived away from home tend to be more mature than those who have not.

A new and welcome Teaching Quality Information (TQI) website (www.tqi.ac.uk), launched in September 2005, aims to provide prospective students with far more information about each university's performance than they've ever had before. The website incorporates a survey of final-year students (170,000 in 2005 – 60% of those eligible) who were asked to rate their courses on 22 factors. Among other things, the findings will enable you to identify the good and the bad. Unfortunately, students at Oxford, Cambridge and Warwick organised resistance to the survey, so there are no meaningful findings for these universities. In addition to the survey findings, the TQI website provides a lot of other relevant information.

However, the TQI website provides only limited, and sometimes dated, information relating to Scottish universities. Scottish final-year students are not included in the survey of final-year students. In Scotland there are separate arrangements for surveying student satisfaction. You can find more at www.mori.com/ontrack Sadly, this offers little information helpful to those choosing a course, and the survey deliberately prevents any comparisons being made between universities.

It is argued that another measure of quality is the quality of research being done in a department. This can have an important bearing on the content of courses. At first-degree level this is not proven, and it is probably more important for postgraduate study. The Quality Assurance Agency for Higher Education (QAA) assesses departments on the quality of research on a seven-point scale from 1 up to 5* (level 3 is subdivided into two).

A book that usefully brings together the currently available assessments and other helpful guidance is *The Guardian University Guide* produced in association with Campus Pi at Brunel University. You could also look at the Guardian's online university guide (http://education.guardian. co.uk/guides/).

Also check courses with your careers teacher, or look them up in the current edition of the UCAS 'Big Guide'. At the start of this chapter, I said that plenty of people would be offering you advice. It is always worth listening. However, I do stress that the final decision has to be yours. You have to take ownership of your own career – your degree choice is the first major step you take on that path.

Key points to think about

You might like to discuss these points with your parents, a guardian or friends.

■ Employers value most arts and humanities disciplines.

■ Rates of unemployment are higher among people with arts and humanities degrees than among people with other degree disciplines.

■ The best reason for choosing a particular subject is personal interest.

■ Interests and aptitudes can be tested as a guide to career choice.

■ Universities offer a far wider subject choice than schools.

■ Courses with the same name differ widely in content between universities.

■ Combined courses are increasingly popular because of their flexibility.

■ Studying away from home costs more, but matures you and can offer better job prospects.

■ You need good objective advice, but then you must make your own choice of degree course.

Chapter three
Trends in graduate employment

When people of your parents' age were graduating, graduates were an elite. They were only one in twenty of new entrants to the workforce. And most of them entered the professions, university teaching, the senior grades of the Civil Service, or management traineeships with major companies. Today the number graduating each year has increased eightfold, and approaching half of all school leavers (43%) now enter higher education. The idea that graduates are an elite has gone for ever.

Moreover, in recent years our economy has undergone a massive restructuring to make us more competitive in world markets. This 'post-industrial revolution' has in many ways been just as profound as the industrial revolution of the 18th and 19th centuries, but largely accomplished in a much shorter time. The growth industries are those that either create and manufacture products that exploit the latest science and technology, or those that provide services to organisations and individuals. These services range from consultancy to financial services, hotels to healthcare, entertainment to retailing, advertising to public administration. The original industrial revolution was skill based; the post-industrial revolution is knowledge based. Twenty years ago the number of 'white collar' knowledge-based jobs in Britain overtook the number of skill-based 'blue collar' jobs for the first time – and the gap has been widening ever since.

How are jobs changing?

As old industries die and new ones are born, there are many changes in the way people work. Most manual jobs have been replaced by machines, and most routine clerical work, by computers. On the other hand, the use of increasingly complex technology has created large numbers of jobs for specialists of various kinds. Most jobs now are 'white collar' knowledge-based jobs, and the proportion is continually rising.

Moreover, many existing jobs have become more complex and need greater intellectual skills. As a result, many careers that until quite recently were open to school-leavers – such as chartered accountancy, librarianship, banking, journalism, personnel and the commissioned ranks of the Armed Forces – are now largely graduate entry.

The way in which work is organised is also changing, and this too is affecting graduate careers.

How are graduates affected?

The traditional graduate career was fairly predictable. You'd probably have been taken on by one of a small number of big employers, having joined as a trainee on the assumption that you'd got a job for life. Your training programme, lasting about two years, would have led to your first proper management post. Your career development would then have been by regular moves up the promotion ladder, in jobs of increasing seniority, which took you up through the many ranks in the management pyramid.

However, employers have had to cut costs and become more efficient to meet growing competition at home and overseas. So they've stripped out whole layers of management, often leaving only four or five levels from the most junior positions through to the very top. They have also cut staffing to the bone, so that British workers are said to work the longest hours in Europe. Moreover, the Institute for Employment Studies has found that graduates in higher-level occupations tend to work longer hours than non-graduates, especially in mid-career.

As well as growing competition, the pace of change is accelerating. If organisations are to survive they must adapt to these changes quickly. Let me give a few examples.

- New competitors appear out of nowhere on the internet and steal customers – as happened in travel, book and CD retailing.

- The entry of supermarkets into banking, financial and travel services, petrol sales, dry cleaning, pharmacy and other areas, created new rivals for existing businesses.

- Microsoft took only 15 years from its start to becoming the world's most valuable business.

- Customers and investors no longer buy only on quality and price, but are now influenced by ecological, ethical and other 'issue' considerations.

In today's climate of rapid change and growing complexity all employees, including graduates, need to work and be trained, developed and managed in new ways. This means constant reorganisation. This is not confined to industry and commerce; the public sector too is going through constant change. A series of surveys in recent years suggests that almost two-thirds of all large organisations go through some form of reorganisation in any one year. These changes affect graduate careers in five ways.

- There are fewer openings in big organisations, but more in small businesses.

- There are new ways of working and fewer opportunities for promotion.

- Although 'permanent jobs' are still the norm, a significant number of people are employed on contracts that offer less long-term job security.

- The number of 'management training schemes' is static, in spite of the huge growth in the economy and in graduate supply.

- Few employers now provide career planning, so graduates must take responsibility for their own career development.

A wider range of non-traditional openings

With far smaller management structures, large employers will never again need the numbers of traditional graduate management trainees that they have in the past. Although large organisations do still recruit small numbers of high-calibre management trainees, far more are now recruited directly into either specialist functions or into lower-level jobs in which they are expected to make an immediate contribution.

Medium and small companies have recently started to recruit graduates for the first time. This has created a wide range of new opportunities. These often provide a wider variety of duties than is traditionally found in a large organisation. However, those recruited as an organisation's first graduates can have some initial problems because the employer tends either to underestimate or overestimate their abilities.

'Graduates are far more likely than people without degrees to find their way into managerial, professional or associate professional occupations. Not only are graduate salaries higher than those earned by non-graduates with the same number of years in the labour market, but graduate salary progression is also faster throughout their early and mid-careers. Even when graduates in higher-level occupations are compared with non-graduates doing similar work, graduates earn more.'

Institute for Employment Studies

New ways of working and fewer opportunities for promotion

The traditional graduate job normally involves working in one place and being responsible for a clear set of duties set out in a 'job description'. You report to one person (your boss), and may have several people reporting to you. You are part of your manager's team, and in turn usually lead your own team. Some graduate jobs are still like this, but they are becoming fewer.

A study for the Association of Graduate Recruiters (AGR) points out that there is a move towards organising much of the work to be done into projects. Each project is carried out by a team appointed on the basis of the skills and knowledge needed until the job is finished. These teams are usually multidisciplinary. Teams form when projects start and disperse when they end.

In this type of work you move from one project to another, and sometimes work on more than one at a time. On some, you may be the leader because the job needs your particular expertise; on others you will be a member of a team led by someone else. You will move through a series of multidimensional roles, rather than a series of rigidly defined jobs. As you perform better and become more expert your pay should improve, but promotion in the traditional sense – another rung on the ladder – will not automatically follow. The regular promotions of the past will be replaced by more flexible but less predictable career paths.

'The structures which have traditionally supported rational long-term careers are being gradually replaced by more fluid organisations... managers' future careers scenarios will be very different from the popular 'onward and upward' view.'

Chartered Institute of Management

There is also a developing need for specialists, but these tend not to manage other staff. Some are employed in consultancy roles, sometimes on a self-employed basis. These jobs need high levels of specialised knowledge. However, a growing proportion of graduate jobs require a portfolio of transferable skills that can be applied in a variety of situations and roles. The knowledge content of these jobs tends to be less specialised, but what you do know needs constant updating. This is one reason why you hear a lot about the importance of 'lifelong learning'.

'Like actors, perhaps, graduates will find that their success will eventually depend on building up a repertoire: using a solid foundation of knowledge and professional skill, then alternating between learning new roles and performing them with increasingly high standards of accomplishment.'

Carol Goodman, AGR study

For arts and humanities graduates, there is good news in the new flexibility. As employers outside science and technology need fewer graduates with specialist knowledge and more with general intellectual and work related key skills, they are opening up more of their vacancies to graduates of 'any discipline'. Around two-thirds of graduate vacancies are now open to graduates of any discipline.

Fewer jobs for life?

You have probably heard that employers can no longer offer a 'job for life'. And certainly far fewer graduates than in the past are likely to develop their entire careers in one organisation. Employment contracts for a fixed length of time, or to complete a specific project, have also become more common. But it appears that the pendulum has started to swing back again. Employers have now recognised that a workforce consisting mostly of contract workers and various kinds of temporary staff does not provide the continuity of effort, consistency of aims and the solid foundation of expertise needed for long-term development. Many employers are now offering increased numbers of permanent posts and some have also begun to accept responsibility for their employees' career development once again.

Fewer management training schemes

In recent years it has been accepted that most graduates will not be employed by the same organisation for the whole of their working lives. Because of this, only a few employers can afford to invest in two-year training programmes for their graduate recruits before they start to see a return for their money. Today most graduates are expected to 'hit the ground running' and make an early contribution. Even in their first year, graduates are given real work that is important to the business. This means that employers expect greater maturity in their recruits and that they are giving graduates responsibility earlier.

Outdated knowledge

Once your full-time education is completed you should have a hefty portfolio of up-to-date knowledge and skills. At one time you could have been fairly confident that this would have been enough to see you through your working life. Unfortunately, the time in which knowledge and skills are getting past their 'use by date' is shrinking rapidly. In 1970 it was calculated that the sum of human knowledge was doubling every 14 years; now it is estimated to double every 18 months.

How this affects people at work is illustrated by the United States Department of Labor. This shows that technological change and new knowledge requirements have cut the 'half-life of skills' (the time in which workers lose half their competence) from between seven and fourteen years in the late 1960s, to between five and seven years by the late 1980s. And, as the pace of change continues its rapid acceleration, the 'half-life of skills' is shrinking even further.

It is obvious that most if not all workers today need their knowledge and skills updating from time to time, so it is not surprising that there is now a strong emphasis on the need for 'lifelong learning'. It is important to individuals to maintain their employability, and for employers to have a workforce that is abreast of current trends and techniques in order to retain and improve their competitiveness.

Employers usually provide induction and skills training, mainly in employees' early employment. But they vary in how well they follow this up. Some think this is enough for an individual's entire career – although it is not. On the other hand, many employers hold annual appraisals to identify training needs for the following year. However, this normally focuses on meeting existing needs, rather than anticipating long-term requirements.

Many employers consider that 'career development' is now the responsibility of the employee. Consequently, employees are expected to identify their own weaknesses and to ask for appropriate training support. Employers prefer to spend their training budget on people they believe are self-motivated to learn. But how can employees anticipate the knowledge and skills that the organisation might need beyond the immediate future?

Career development

With the pace of change, and the speed with which new knowledge outdates the old, 'lifelong learning' is now essential. Many professions formalise this as continuing professional development (CPD), continuing professional education (CPE), or continuing vocational training (CVT). In many professions this is mandatory.

'While it is important for a company or country to have a highly skilled workforce and a strong flow of highly qualified new entrants, it is also essential that their skills and competencies are regularly updated.'

Institute for Employment Studies

In traditional organisations there were clear career paths, and employers accepted responsibility for career development. However, the future is now far less predictable, fewer employers now offer lifetime careers, and people follow much more varied paths. Most employers today expect their staff to take responsibility for their own career development. In practice, this usually means that the organisation will provide training and development when people want it, but it is for employees to identify their own training and development needs and persuade the employer of the validity of their needs. These needs do not just relate to the work that is being done for that employer.

Because jobs are perceived to be less secure, some employers recognise that these training needs may also be concerned with improving the individual's employability in the outside jobs market.

New types of job

Do all these changes mean fewer graduate jobs? No. Although large employers now have fewer 'management trainee' vacancies, this loss of opportunity is more than made up for by new openings in small and medium-sized companies. Some want to strengthen their management team, some need technical specialists, others recruit graduates into roles once held by school-leavers but which have become more complex. If you do aspire to a management traineeship you will find that recruiters will focus on your potential as a leader.

'Generally…the selection criteria [for high potential entry] focus on clusters of competencies seen as critical to leadership:

- intellectual ability, linked to analytical skills and strategic thinking

- interpersonal skills, seen as linked both to influencing skills and the future ability to manage and motivate staff

- drive to achieve results, seen as linked to personal effectiveness.'

'Fishing for talent in a wider pool: trends and dilemmas in corporate graduate recruitment', Institute for Employment Studies, 2005

Large employers, although recruiting fewer management trainees than in the past, now take growing numbers of graduates straight into posts for which they already have appropriate skills. This is more common with scientists and technologists than arts and humanities graduates. But employers also recruit graduates into work once done by school-leavers. It is not that there are fewer graduate jobs, but that the nature of many jobs is changing. Employers now need a larger proportion of their workforce to be highly educated.

Is underemployment a real risk?

Many graduates today enter jobs previously undertaken by A level school-leavers. This has led some people to worry that graduates may end up 'underemployed' in dead-end jobs. However, school-leaver entrants usually worked under close supervision. Graduates are expected to be self-starters who manage their own work. This means they are able to develop the jobs in ways which school-leavers could not, and put their own stamp on them.

Moreover, as jobs become more complex, they increasingly need the skills that graduates can bring to them. Many careers that were mainly school-leaver entry have now become graduate-entry jobs, and this trend will continue.

Some of the newer graduate employers have little experience in training and developing graduates or giving young people early responsibility. (Others could, of course, go the other way and ask too much of young graduates too soon.) It'll be up to you to prove your worth. Make the most of every learning opportunity. Accept responsibility and make something special of any job you're given, however mundane it may at first appear.

Some graduates do find themselves in dead-end jobs. When you're job-seeking start early and be very selective. If you make a mistake and enter the wrong job don't moan about it, but do everything as well as you can and learn as much as possible from the experience before moving on after a year or two.

What of graduate unemployment?

You've probably heard quite a lot about graduate unemployment, and possibly get the impression that many graduates remain unemployed. This is not true. Even in the last recession unemployment among all graduates was only half the level of that among people with good GCSEs, and only a quarter of that of people with no qualifications. The job market, including that for graduates, follows the economy. In the past this swung from recession to boom and back again roughly every five years. But the market has become more stable. But even during the last recession, one in eight members of the AGR was unable to fill all their vacancies. This isn't to say they didn't get enough applicants, but the AGR says they lacked applicants with good interpersonal skills and business awareness.

It is widely agreed by employers and graduate careers advisory services that if undergraduates take their job-search really seriously as they approach graduation, they'll almost certainly find a job. The keys to success are:

- develop your transferable or key skills (see Chapter four)

- make full use of your university's careers advisory service

- start applying for jobs at the start of your third year – no later

- take advantage of employers' campus visits (the 'milkround')

- monitor job advertisements aimed at final-year undergraduates – on the internet, in *Prospects* and in the press

- target your applications carefully – the scatter-gun approach doesn't work

- apply only to organisations for whom you'd really like to work

- don't ignore small employers – they get fewer applications

- make sure applications are well presented.

Although only a minority of vacancies are filled through employers' milkround visits made shortly after Christmas in the final year, this remains the main recruitment market for management trainees by large employers. Yet, surprisingly, many finalists don't bother looking for jobs until the milkround is over, and so miss many, if not most, of the best opportunities. A quarter don't even apply for a single job until after their finals. On the other hand, the two-thirds who start their job search before the Christmas preceding their finals are the most likely to be successful. It is worth noting that those who see themselves as 'high flyers' (with higher than average salary and degree-class expectations and who see themselves as having a certain combination of managerial and motivational qualities) tend to make their choices early and are the most active in applying for jobs. Moreover, a recent survey by the psychometric specialists SHL Group found that undergraduates who are the first to apply on graduate recruitment programmes are more intelligent, energetic, analytical, motivated and forward thinking than those who apply closer to the closing date.

Graduate starting salaries

Finally, it is worth looking at the starting salaries paid to new graduates. It can be misleading to talk of 'average' salaries. A much better way is to use the median, which means 'middle item'. If we take a group of graduates and list them in salary order from the highest paid down to the lowest, the salary of the person halfway down our list is the median.

For those starting work in the autumn of 2005, the median starting salary for a typical newly qualified 21-year-old graduate with a second-class honours degree is £22,500, according to the *AGR Graduate Recruitment Survey 2005 (Summer Review)*. This level of salary is paid to those entering graduate-level jobs. Many graduates, either because they did not start their job-search soon enough or lack the skills that employers are looking for, find themselves competing with non-graduates for vacancies that can pay significantly less.

The AGR surveys, carried out by High Flyers Research each summer and winter, show a wide span between the highest and lowest salaries paid in graduate-level jobs. These ranged from less than £15,000 in one insurance company through to 16 employers (mainly investment banks and legal and consulting firms) offering £35,000 or more.

Clearly, some industries pay more than others. The median salaries that employers in different industries actually offered in 2005 were as follows:

- Hotels and catering £17,000

- Media companies £19,500

- Retail £20,000

- Public sector £22,000

- IT hardware or software £22,000

- Energy, water and utilities £22,000

- Accountancy and professional services £22,000

- Banking and financial services £23,000

- Fast-moving consumer goods £24,500

- Armed Forces £25,600

- Consultancy £28,500

- Investment banking £35,000.

Academic disciplines in short supply command higher salaries, and there are variations by geographical location and by type of work, and so on. Although the salaries listed are unlikely to be directly relevant to you, they do give an indication of pay levels as well as showing that the 'averages' quoted in the press and elsewhere can be highly misleading.

Key points to think about

You might like to discuss these points with your parents, a guardian or friends.

- Employment patterns are changing fundamentally.

- There are fewer traditional graduate traineeships.

- There are more non-traditional jobs for graduates.

- There are fewer promotions in the average career path.

- Career progress is achieved through flexibility and mobility.

- Underemployment in non-traditional graduate jobs is likely to be relatively rare.

- Graduates have lower unemployment rates than other workers.

- The search for a job should start early in the final academic year.

■ Few arts and humanities graduates enter work directly relevant to their degree, except teaching.

■ The most important factor in career choice is 'intellectual challenge'.

Chapter four
Adding value to your degree

Until a few years ago most employers recruited non-technical graduates as management trainees destined for top jobs. If you had graduated then, you would typically have joined a training programme lasting from one to two years. This would have involved going on courses, starting to study for a professional qualification and doing project work in several departments.

This experience in various departments, often known as the 'Cook's Tour', would develop your work-related skills, help you to understand how the organisation operated as a whole and find out what type of work suited you best. It was only after this lengthy preparation that you'd normally start a real job and begin to work your way up the promotion ladder. Today few start in this way.

'There is a growing recognition of the need to enhance graduates' employability for them to find suitable jobs in an increasingly diverse and competitive labour market. The 'employability' debate has centred on the adequacy of the skills graduates develop during their courses. There is growing consensus that it is no longer sufficient for graduates to possess traditional academic and subject-specific skills. Nowadays graduates need to develop a range of interpersonal and transferable skills to be able to adapt to changing market circumstances and organisational needs.'

'The Art of Getting Started: Graduate skills in a fragmented labour market', Institute for Employment Studies, 2005

It is the acquisition of these interpersonal and transferable skills that 'add value' to your degree and so make you more employable. Because of the changes described in the last chapter the number of employers seeking 'high flyers' for management traineeships has at best remained static. On the other hand, employers recruit graduates into a far wider range of jobs. Employers expect graduates to develop their careers by moving between various types of work of increasing complexity and responsibility. Although graduates still get good training, most are also expected to do real work almost from the beginning. They are expected to make a real contribution to the business and earn their pay as soon as possible.

These changes mean that employers are changing their recruitment criteria. Once it would have been enough to have a good degree, to be polite and well-groomed, and to show an interest in the job and a willingness to learn. These qualities are still valued but they are no longer enough. Employers now look for evidence that you've also got some of the key skills (also known as core skills in Scotland, or as competencies or employability skills) that will help you to make an early and successful transition from education to employment. Before we look in detail at the skills you will need, it is helpful to understand how the way you work as a student differs from how you will work once you are employed.

Study and work: the differences

As a student you work to a known syllabus. All the information you need, and guidance on the reliability of your sources, is normally to hand. If you have an essay or project to do, you usually have ample time to complete it and so can work at your own pace. Much student work is done alone and to personal targets. If you do work with others, perhaps on a project, it is probably with a peer group of your own choice. The aim of your studies is to be able to give 'ideal answers' to set problems. The answers you produce and the essays you write are the end products of your efforts.

At work you are in a far less certain world. Your activities are increasingly unlikely to be tied to a fixed 'job specification' setting out your responsibilities and duties. The environment in which your employers operate will be constantly changing. All organisations are undergoing evolution. The most successful are those that are flexible and can adapt fastest to changing circumstances. Similarly, the most successful people in these organisations are those who are similarly flexible and adaptable.

Given problems to solve at work, you'll seldom have all the information needed to arrive at 'ideal answers' or enough time to evaluate all the data you have before you have to offer a solution. In addition, you can't always verify the reliability of your sources. You must use your judgement and offer the best answer you can in the time available. Often you'll work on several problems at once. At work, your answers won't be an end in themselves but the basis on which decisions involving people, money and time will be made. Many decisions cannot be reversed – even if better solutions turn up later. You'll have to live with your decisions and do your best to make them work.

You'll almost certainly work in a team of people of different ages and disciplines, aiming at shared objectives. Because team members depend on one another to achieve results, you will need good interpersonal skills and must understand how your work fits in with that of your team colleagues and of the organisation as a whole.

Developing key skills

According to the Association of Graduate Recruiters (AGR) the skills and personal attributes that employers look for in newly qualified graduates are, in order of importance:

- motivation and enthusiasm

- interpersonal skills

- team working

- oral communication

- flexibility and adaptability

- initiative and proactivity

- problem solving

- planning and organisation

- managing your own development

- written communication

- customer orientation

- time management

- business awareness

- numeracy (application of number)

- leadership

- cultural sensitivity

- general IT/computer literacy

- risk taking/entrepreneurship

- foreign languages.

At school you should have come across some of these under the six 'key skills' that are part of the National Vocational Qualifications – communication, application of number, IT, working with others, improving own learning and performance, and problem solving. (In Scotland you should have come across the five 'core skills' – much the same as the key skills in the rest of the UK except for improving your own learning and performance). But as you can see, graduate employers hope for a lot more. To have some of the more important skills helps you to win your first job, move easily from student life into work, and helps to ensure your long-term employability. You can also move more easily from one type of work to another, and from one employer to another.

They are valuable anywhere – in a profession, industry, commerce, public service, the Armed Forces or the voluntary sector. (N.B. Working in the voluntary sector is not the same as doing voluntary work – voluntary work is unpaid but organisations that use volunteers often employ staff in various functions.) Many of these skills are also useful in private life. Because they have broad application they have been called transferable skills, but today they tend to be called 'key' or 'core' skills.

Employers won't expect you to join them from full-time education with these skills fully developed. What they will look for is evidence that you have got a basic grounding in some of them. You could acquire some through your academic work at school and university, through recreational activities including voluntary work, through paid employment, holiday work and work placements and through special training courses. Let us take a look at some of these skills in more detail.

Interpersonal skills

Simply, this means getting on with people. Whether you work with customers, colleagues at all levels, suppliers or anyone else – you must be able to work comfortably with them and earn their respect and trust. This means having good social skills. You don't have to be an extrovert or the 'life and soul of the party', but you do need a friendly manner and to develop reasonable conversational skills. You also have to show a real interest in other people, be considerate and good mannered with them, be a willing listener, offer help when it is needed, and accept your share of any joint task. You need to avoid conflict and when disagreements occur, avoid blaming others for your mistakes, and be willing to accept compromise when necessary. And if you are wrong, apologise without qualification. It's also OK to be assertive, but never be aggressive.

Team working

Most work today is carried out by people working in multidisciplinary teams. In a team, your personal objectives must take second place to those of the group. You must see how your work fits in with that of your colleagues and of the organisation as a whole. You must combine the ability to argue your point of view persuasively with the willingness to listen and learn from others and to make compromises when necessary. It helps to be cheerful, unselfish and loyal to the team. Taking part in team sports and other group pursuits is good preparation. Employment experience that involves working with others is especially valuable. So too are such activities as scouting or guiding, Raleigh International, the Duke of Edinburgh's Award scheme and personal development courses, such as those run by Outward Bound and other outdoor development training centres.

Oral communication

This is a vital skill in almost all workplaces. Watch how people pass on information, instructions and ideas. Note what they do well – and badly! Use them as examples and warnings. At school and university you get lots of opportunities to do this. Practise your oral communication skills in discussions, debates, answering questions, organising student events and in general conversation. Again, aim for clarity and brevity. You can also learn a lot from chairing meetings for a club or society – making announcements, introducing items on the agenda, controlling the discussion, summarising the points made, trying to get a consensus view and introducing and thanking guest speakers. Also aim to be an attentive listener.

The more frequently you hear yourself say 'you know what I mean', the more you need to work at your communication skills. A simple and very effective method, but easy to forget, is to get into the habit of pausing for a second or two to set your ideas in order before you speak. The old advice 'think before you speak' can't be bettered. And if you have to make a presentation, open a debate, attend an interview and so on, think the whole thing through carefully.

Problem solving

Much student work involves finding an answer to a set problem from many possibilities. This isn't a matter of trial and error (or shouldn't be) but a systematic process in which you draw on your knowledge and experience to come up with possible solutions. This is the process of reasoning. It's a creative process that can be used equally well in student or working life to deal with theoretical or practical problems. Think carefully about the way in which you tackle work or other activities.

'No problem can be solved with the same consciousness that created it. Today's problems are yesterday's solution.'

Albert Einstein, scientist

Managing your own development

Most employers today expect you to identify your own training needs (see Chapter three), and then they will provide the appropriate training and work experience when asked. Many people today, especially graduates, prepare a Personal Development Plan (PDP). This is a clear and succinct summary of your short- and medium-term career plans, your personal learning needs to achieve those plans, and an action plan to meet them. At its simplest it is used by people to review the skills they need in their current job or sometimes for the next rung up the ladder. But a PDP is far more useful if it forms the nucleus of a wider career plan – establishing medium- to long-term objectives, setting out alternative strategies because the future is never wholly predictable, identifying your learning needs, and setting out a plan of self-development.

Written communication skills

Whatever subject you choose to specialise in, you really should develop your skill in using the English language. Occasionally you'll have to explain your work, however specialised, to non-specialists and people of other disciplines. Try to develop a writing style in which you present information and ideas in logical order, clearly and succinctly. When necessary, you should also be able to argue a case persuasively. Apart from jobs in publishing and advertising, most writing at work involves form-filling, memoranda (brief notes either giving instructions, passing on information, asking questions or answering queries), emails, letters and writing reports.

Clarity and brevity are more important than 'literary' style. Many students who have written up experiments in physics or chemistry find this a good preparation for structuring essays and reports. Acting as secretary to a club or society – producing agendas, minuting meetings and writing letters – is valuable practice.

Errors of grammar and spelling are never acceptable at work. No employer will want you to offend educated colleagues, customers or suppliers – or distract them from the message – by the incorrect use of English. Although word-processing packages have spell-checkers, people often forget to set them to UK English instead of US English spelling. Moreover, they check only to see that a word is in the dictionary and ignore the context. Having commented on the trap this creates for the unwary in her *Daily Telegraph* column, Alison Eadie received the following from an unnamed source:

> That's awl rite
> Eye have a spelling chequer
> It came with my pea sea
> It plainly marques four my revue
> Mistakes eye cannot sea
> I've run this poem threw it
> I'm sure your pleas too no
> Its letter perfect in it's weigh
> My chequer tolled me sew.

You still need to know your spelling. The best means to acquire good English is to read critically. Analyse what writers do to get their ideas across.

'For a man to write well, there are required three necessaries – to read the best authors, observe the best speakers, and much exercise in his own style.'

Ben Jonson, Elizabethan dramatist

Customer orientation

Employers in all fields, not just commercial firms, focus their activities on the customer. They will welcome proof of your interest in and understanding of other people. Ideally, you should have experience of providing customer service – meeting the needs of others. Serving people in a shop, student union, café, hotel or other service industry is extremely valuable. You should learn how to make people feel genuinely welcome, ask questions to find out what they want, answer queries and explain things, persuade them that you can satisfy their needs, and handle any complaints. When you are a customer, observe how staff treat you and communicate with you. Note what they do that you particularly like and dislike.

Customer orientation also means meeting the needs of 'internal customers'. Even if you are not in direct contact with customers, somewhere up or down the line from you are people who are. They can only satisfy the needs of external customers if you, and everyone else backing them up, meet their needs. So whenever you do something for someone, think of them as your customer and do your best to satisfy their needs – so that they in turn can satisfy the needs of those further down the line.

Time management

As a student you're used to completing pieces of work, such as essays, by a set date. Working like this to 'deadlines' is normal at work. At times you may have several assignments at once, some more important than others, each with its own deadline. Effective time management first involves prioritising the relative importance of the various tasks you've got to complete and the order in which they should be carried out. Then you must use the normally limited time you've got available as effectively as you can. You have to decide how much time to give to each task and then keep to your timetable so that you can meet all the deadlines.

Graduate recruiters often test these skills, and others, at an assessment centre as the final stage of their selection process. They test your ability to prioritise work and manage your time with a written 'in-tray exercise'. This simulates a typical pile of papers that might face you at work. You have to decide your priorities, maybe delegate some items (but not too many), and then carry out the other tasks. These may include writing memos and letters.

Business awareness

If you're choosing arts or humanities because you think this is a way to escape the world of commercial values, you'll almost certainly be disappointed. It isn't only that industry and commerce are the biggest employers of arts and humanities graduates. Whatever field you enter – public service, charity, or even the creative and performing arts – your work will be affected one way or another by business factors. You'll have 'customers' with needs to satisfy, whether they pay or not. In an art gallery your customers are the viewing public; in a school, the pupils; in a hospital, the patients; and in a theatre, the audience. Often you can have two sets of customers. So, in an employment agency one set of customers are the employers with jobs to fill; the other customers being the job seekers.

It costs money to run any sort of enterprise. This money must be raised in some way, whether by selling goods or a service, raising taxes or soliciting charitable donations. Income and expenditure must be budgeted and accounted for. All the laws about property, employing people, health and safety, insurance, environmental protection, consumer rights and much more must be observed. Get some practical work experience. Evening, weekend and holiday work won't just help your finances (especially while at university) but will provide experience that graduate recruiters value highly. Take any available opportunities to visit employers or go 'work-shadowing' (observing someone in their daily working routine). If there is a family business, learn what you can from it.

When you're at work, even in a mundane job, you can learn a lot by watching, listening and asking the right questions. Ask yourself why your work is organised as it is and how it fits into the overall scheme of things. What skills do you find are most important in your job? What would be the consequences for the business of different sorts of mistake? How could they be rectified? Observe how managers succeed, or fail, to get the willing support of their team. The graduate recruiters you meet eventually are going to be very interested in how much you consciously learned from your work experiences.

If you wonder if a career in management might suit you after taking a degree, it is well worth going on an Insight into Management Course run by the Careers Research Advisory Centre (CRAC) and by some university careers advisory services. This will substantially improve your business awareness and give you an insight into how managers think and work. You would undertake a variety of projects and exercises, usually to tight deadlines, under the guidance of young managers from industry. These courses are enjoyable as well as being highly regarded by employers. Your careers teacher should be able to give you more information.

Once at university, check *as soon as possible* with your careers service for work experience opportunities (the best soon go) and get any details of business awareness days, introductory management courses run by employers (usually over the Christmas or Easter vacations), work shadowing opportunities, vacation employment, and key or core skills programmes. Your own university may run a further CRAC Insight into Management activity that you could attend. And if you're interested in a management career in industry or commerce, it's a good idea to join the Student Industrial Society at your university. This organisation runs activities, often with employer support, which will give you information about and experience of the business world.

Numeracy

Almost all graduate jobs involve using figures at times. Don't worry if maths turns you off and you think you're innumerate. The maths most employers want involves simple but accurate arithmetic and a little common sense.

You should be able to add, subtract, multiply, divide and work out percentages fairly quickly and with consistent accuracy – preferably without a calculator. These are the most common calculations you'll meet at work.

Statistical information is used by all kinds of employer and in almost every type of graduate work from time to time. You should be able to interpret information involving numbers, whether in the form of statistical tables, graphs, or bar and other kinds of charts. Statistics can be misleading. They seldom tell direct lies but often conceal the truth. Mark Twain cynically warned:

'There are three kinds of lies – lies, damned lies and statistics.'

Mark Twain

Let's take two examples from fictitious advertisements.

'Nine out of ten men use Aqua Regia aftershave.'

This is less likely to mean 'nine men in every ten' than 'nine of the ten men we chose specially'.

'The earnings of our twenty sales staff average £40,000 a year.'

This could mean that three senior sales people with good territories each earn £175,000 a year, but the other seventeen only get £16,175 a year. The statement is true – but highly misleading!

Statistics, used properly, are valuable and reliable. If you see them quoted to support an argument – especially by advertisers, salespeople and politicians – try to spot any loopholes. This will help your numeracy, improve your powers of judgement and make you a discriminating shopper and voter. And it can be fun!

It is also useful, if slightly more difficult, to understand the idea of probability – the laws of chance. Statisticians use probability to work out the likelihood of a particular occurrence taking place.

Leadership

There is little agreement concerning what makes a good leader, and there are also different leadership styles. But most people, including employers, agree that leadership is not about using your status to boss other people about.

Chapter three explains that work groups today are often formed, dissolved and regrouped to suit the projects in hand. As a result, the team leadership may move from one person to another as the project changes. In these situations, you can expect to move in and out of leadership roles without changing your formal status.

The most effective leader, particularly in today's flexible organisation, is likely to be the person everyone turns to when they need guidance and support. This type of leader gets the willing effort of others, motivates them to do their best and earns the team's respect – usually through a combination of personal example, knowledge, enthusiasm, tact, decisiveness, tenacity and, above all, integrity. Rank and status are largely irrelevant.

There are certain basic qualities that have always been needed to lead a team of people successfully in the long-term. These are:

- good communication skills

- good listening skills

- honesty and trustworthiness

- understanding of what motivates people

- clear vision of the team's objectives

- finds challenge exciting

- accepts personal responsibility

- problem-solving skills

- ability to delegate
- see jobs through to completion
- mental toughness
- recognises and praises the contribution of others
- ensures that any criticism of others is fair and constructive
- acknowledges own mistakes
- constant willingness to learn.

'When the best leader's work is done, the people say 'we did it ourselves'.'

Lao-Tzu, Chinese philosopher, 6th century BC

Get as much experience as you can of working within a team – first just as a member. You won't be able to lead until you understand how teams work together. Your future employers will welcome any experience you've had as a prefect or house captain, leader in the Scouts or Guides Associations, sports team captain or in similar roles.

Employers also value any experience in running student or club events. If it includes coordinating the work of volunteer helpers and working within a budget and to a strict timetable, even better. However, serving on school or university committees and holding office is valued only if you take an active role. Employers and university admissions staff are fully aware that some students start societies and committees just so that they can put them in their application forms.

Cultural sensitivity

Many employers are now multinationals or trade internationally. And even entirely domestic organisations often have employees drawn from a wide variety of cultural backgrounds. You don't want to give offence through ignorance or making false assumptions. This is far easier that you might think. Book a Japanese visitor into a hotel room with a four in the number, serve beef to a Hindu, or offer a gift to someone from the Middle East with your left hand and you will offend them all! Overseas travel and reading appropriate books will help (especially recommended is *Riding the Waves of Culture*, published by Nicholas Brealey).

Information and computer technology

In 1977, in the lifetime of your own parents, the president of DEC (Digital Equipment Corporation) said: 'There is no reason for anyone to have a computer in their home.' A generation before that, in 1943, the Chairman of IBM said: 'I think there is a world market for about five computers.' Yet, in a single generation, computers have revolutionised jobs and leisure. The changes likely to occur in your own working life are impossible to forecast – but they will be huge.

At present the main uses of computers at work, outside science and engineering, are for filing and accessing of information (databases); desk research (externally through the internet and internally through intranets); the transmission and receipt of information to and from customers, suppliers and colleagues (emails and their attachments); entering and manipulating figures including financial data (spreadsheets); and for typing and storing the written word (word-processing). Graphics and desktop publishing packages are widely used, and designers now make extensive use of CAD (computer-aided design).

You'll use computers during your university course. University facilities range from PCs through to 'supercomputers'. As well as writing your essays, you can conduct academic research through the internet, which provides access to vast libraries of electronically stored information worldwide.

Foreign languages

Although British recruiters rarely ask for languages, many organisations lose business because they lack the necessary language skills. This is likely to change in the not too distant future. Having language skills may not help you much at the recruitment stage, but is likely to give you a distinct edge in a few years' time. Many arts and humanities courses include a modern language option that involves a year abroad. There are also opportunities to study for part of your second year at a university in mainland Europe, for example through schemes such as ERASMUS, part of the SOCRATES programme organised by the European Commission. Your university may also offer language laboratory or other facilities for voluntary spare-time language learning.

Exchange visits with overseas students, school trips (as long as you talk to the locals, not just your own party) and overseas holidays can all develop your language skills. Listen to overseas radio, or try reading newspapers/ magazines from other countries and, as you improve, include books.

Key skills and university courses

The Government and employers have encouraged universities to incorporate key skills training into their courses. Support is still uneven, and even in a single university there can be big differences between departments. It's worth seeking out courses that incorporate key skills training. They are just as rigorous academically as other courses, but can give you the bonus of skills for which employers are looking, and which you'll find personally valuable. Allied to these courses, many universities run short programmes to develop specific key skills.

Work experience

It is official Government policy that every undergraduate should have worthwhile work experience while at university. Work experience is highly valued by employers and is often a prerequisite for graduate employment. Unfortunately, there are not enough 'worthwhile' student jobs for everyone. It is sensible to look for suitable work experience opportunities as soon as you get to university or college (ideally during 'freshers' week'). Even if you eventually can only get mundane work, don't underestimate the value of the lessons to be learned from it.

Even if you end up with a Saturday job in a retail shop, or doing bar work in the student union, you will learn valuable lessons in such things as customer care and handling cash. Employers are often more interested in the lessons you learned from what you did than they are in the type of work you carried out.

Jake Eliot

Jake, 23, shows how gaining work experience helped him to develop his career ideas and provided him with valuable experience to offer to employers.

Career profile

Job title: policy and research assistant

Employer: National Council for Voluntary Organisations (NCVO)

A levels: history, politics, economics and general studies

Degree: BA modern history

University: St. Hugh's College, Oxford

'I wanted to do history or politics and something else, and originally thought a joint degree might be to my taste. But the more I thought about it, and chatted to my teachers, the more I realised I should do a straight history degree. This offered more flexibility and freedom, so I'd be able to look at political theory and the history of political thought – the stuff that really interested me.

The course itself is really broad and flexible. During those three years you have to cover one medieval, one early modern and one modern period. Other than that you were free to select your own courses. I ended up specialising in the later 18th century. It was such an important stage for the history of political ideas – the enlightenment, the French revolution and so on.

I tried to leave my career options open. From the sixth form I was very interested in politics and at school was involved in the Model United Nations Programme. So I thought I might go into that general field.

For two summers I worked for the Open University summer schools at Bath University. That was halfway between a temporary job and work experience. It was a really useful opportunity to develop my communication skills with 'customers' and other members of staff.

When I left university I arranged a series of work experience placements. A couple of those were in political consultancies and lobbying firms, and a couple more in press offices. I began looking for jobs concurrently with my work experience.

In early 2004, a couple of temporary job opportunities came up. These ended up as two part-time jobs that I did for a couple of months. One was doing policy research for a very small educational charity – Tools for Schools. That was really interesting. They encouraged big blue-chip firms to donate their old IT systems, which they sold on cheaply to schools to help build up their ICT capacity. The other half of the week was a temporary position as a researcher in the House of Lords. I was researching background issues, writing briefing papers and speeches.

I'd been gradually thinking about policy rather than political consultancy. And working for the voluntary sector had been at the back of my mind as something I'd be very keen to do.

I then saw a job advertised with the National Council for Voluntary Organisations (NCVO) that seemed almost ideal – public policy in the voluntary sector. I was delighted to be offered the job. I've been there just over a year. My job is a small project within a policy team – producing, writing and disseminating briefings, reports and position papers.

One of the things I've become convinced about, in the two years since I left university, is that graduates will have to be more flexible in terms of what we do and how many different types of things we will do during our careers. I have a couple of ideas about where I might like to be in the longer term, but I'm trying to keep the need to be flexible at the forefront of my mind. At the moment I'd really like to stay in the voluntary sector. I really enjoy it and like the ethos.

I suppose the next step up for me would be as a full policy officer somewhere in the voluntary sector. Public affairs campaigning would also really interest me.

A lot of experiences at university are very intense, particularly toward the end of the course. So it is really important to take some sort of pause and think very hard about the sorts of things that you might be interested in, or the sorts of skills that you have and might want to develop. You should keep yourself adaptable and open to new ideas. And once you know what you want to do, carry on applying for jobs. It requires a huge amount of tenacity to keep sending in application forms when you keep getting rejection letter after rejection letter. You need the drive to say: 'this is what I want, and something will come up if I keep putting the applications in and getting some work experience'.'

Key points to think about

You might like to discuss these points with your parents, a guardian or friends:

- A good degree on its own is unlikely to get you a graduate level job.

- Graduate recruiters look for a range of 'transferable' skills.

- Skills gained through practical work experience are especially valued.

- Activities to improve the following are to be encouraged:
  - team working
  - leadership
  - clear and accurate use of spoken and written English
  - problem solving
  - business awareness
  - simple but accurate arithmetic
  - interpretation of statistics
  - computer skills
  - setting work priorities and time management
  - foreign languages and cultural awareness.
- Choose a degree course with key skills content if possible.

Section 2

Graduate careers using your degree subject

This section looks at those careers in which you could make substantial use of your degree subject. However, because many employers are flexible about the specific disciplines they are looking for, I would urge you not to look only at the chapter dealing with your specific discipline. Look carefully at the other chapters as well.

Some subjects are grouped together in one chapter because they offer very similar career opportunities.

Area studies, which include language studies (such as African, Celtic, French, German, Italian, Oriental, Russian and East European, Semitic, and Spanish and Latin American studies), are all covered in Chapter eleven.

Art history is covered in Chapter eight.

Linguistics is also covered in Chapter eleven.

It is important to realise that there are many more arts and humanities graduates than there are job vacancies which need a directly relevant degree discipline. Fortunately, many other careers are open to you. You will probably find that, although you may not use your specialist knowledge, the key skills you acquire in doing your course – such as communication skills, interpersonal skills, and data handling and analytical skills – are highly valued by employers. Careers that do not need your specialist knowledge are covered in Section 3.

Chapter five
Teaching your subject

It's impossible to exaggerate the importance of education. Not only is our economy based more and more on knowledge-based activities, but many global problems that arise from poverty, disease and a shortage of resources will only be solved through the application of knowledge. Moreover, ignorance is often at the root of the prejudice and suspicion behind many of the world's conflicts.

'Human history becomes more and more a race between education and catastrophe.'

H G Wells, English novelist, journalist and sociologist

If education is vitally important, then so is teaching. It seems odd therefore that teaching is not always highly valued as a profession. But undervaluing teachers is nothing new. A hundred years ago the Irish playwright George Bernard Shaw said:

'He who can, does. He who cannot, teaches.'

G B Shaw, Irish playwright

You probably know that there are some well-publicised concerns in the teaching profession. Many teachers complain of being overworked, of not having enough time or resources to do their job properly, of disruption caused by a minority of disruptive pupils, and of suffering from stress. This is true. For years they have also had to cope with a succession of changes in the educational system – changes with which they don't always agree – and this has created an extra burden on what is already often a stressful job. If this looks a bit negative, it's worth remembering that in most professions people have to cope with continual change. Most would like fewer time pressures, better resources and less stress. These issues are not exclusive to the teaching profession!

On the positive side, teaching is a career in which you help young people to develop their full potential. This is both challenging and rewarding. Teaching offers variety and the opportunity to be creative and original. Prospects for promotion are good. The financial rewards can be excellent in the long term. Teachers also enjoy the longest paid holidays of any profession, even taking into account that some of this time is likely to be spent in work-related activities.

Although teachers can work with all ages from infants upwards, graduates teaching the subjects they studied at degree level normally work in secondary schools, or in further or higher education.

After reading this chapter you may decide to abandon the idea of studying for an arts or humanities degree and read for a BEd, BA(Ed) or BA leading to QTS (Qualified Teacher Status) instead. You will be able to specialise at either primary or secondary level. However, do not follow this route unless you are absolutely sure you want to teach. A BEd or BA(Ed) rarely carries the same weight with employers outside teaching as an arts or humanities degree plus a PGCE.

Your work as a teacher

Whether you teach in a school, college or university, there are many common elements in the work you would do. Before looking at these, and then examining the differences, it is worth noting the difference between pupils and students. Pupils are taught by someone else (as they mostly are in school); students spend much or most of their time studying without supervision (as they mostly are in university). For the purposes of this chapter I shall refer to both as students.

Your aim is to help all your students to reach their full potential. This means not only developing their existing abilities, but also looking at their aptitudes and their aspirations.

Before you can teach anything to anyone, you must build a good relationship with the student and find ways to stimulate interest in your subject. Students must be receptive to the ideas and information that you are providing. You can't force knowledge into people who aren't interested.

You'll quickly find out that what enthuses some people, doesn't work with others. You'll be teaching individuals, each one with a different personality and range of aptitudes. You must find ways to reach every person in your class. You must also be able to keep order, sometimes having to cope with disruptive students.

'For every person wishing to teach there are 30 not wanting to be taught.'

W C Sellar and R J Yeatman, British humorists

When you're working with students, you may use a variety of teaching methods such as lecturing in front of a blackboard or interactive whiteboard, leading discussions, giving demonstrations, conducting experiments, organising individual and group projects or going on visits to places of relevant interest.

'Good teachers make the best of a pupil's means; great teachers foresee a pupil's ends.'

Maria Callas, Italian opera singer

Outside your class you will spend many hours preparing lessons, setting and marking student's work, form filling and writing assessments. You may spend time advising students on personal problems, either informally or as their pastoral tutor. You will have administrative duties and will have to attend departmental, curricular and other meetings. Much of this will be done outside normal school hours. Many teachers also get involved in extracurricular activities with students. These range from sports, drama and concerts to overseas trips. Although these aren't a compulsory part of their job, most teachers know that these activities are important and so give their time willingly.

Students are normally working towards formal qualifications, so your teaching must cover the set curriculum. Your students don't want to find themselves in the examination room facing questions on topics you haven't covered properly. You'll have to draw up a syllabus, ensuring that your students have a balanced programme that will enable them to study everything necessary in the time available.

It is often thought that once a teacher has prepared a syllabus, it can be repeated year after year without change. This isn't so. Good teachers are always looking for better ways to cover the curriculum and to incorporate new ideas and knowledge. Moreover, there is an almost constant stream of change, beyond the teacher's control.

This ranges from changes to the curriculum through to a torrent of education initiatives from the Government. One of the biggest challenges in teaching today is coping with all the changes.

The qualities you need

To form good relationships with your students and maintain order you must combine sensitivity to others with patience, good listening skills, tact, fairness and self-confidence. A sense of humour helps; being able to laugh at yourself is especially useful!

'Teaching is live theatre. You're scriptwriter, producer, stage manager, performer... everything! Done well, it's as creative and exciting as any of the performing arts, and has more purpose.'

University lecturer, London

To teach, you need an enthusiasm for your subject, and must be able to organise information and ideas logically and then communicate them clearly. You must fire the imagination of your students and encourage them to take an active part in their own learning. 'Chalk and talk' is not enough.

'We all like some people more than others. That's only human. But as a teacher I can't have any favourites. This doesn't mean I treat everyone exactly the same. Each youngster is unique and needs individual attention. I want each of my students to know I take a personal interest in them and will always treat them fairly and always do my best for them.'

Teacher, Leicester

To plan a balanced syllabus, prepare lessons, set and mark assignments, and keep to your schedule, you need to be well organised and good at managing your time.

You spend much of the day on your feet in front of your students. You may also have to walk long distances between classes, often carrying heavy loads of books, papers and equipment. The work itself can be stressful. To maintain your enthusiasm you need plenty of energy and stamina – physical, mental and emotional.

Teaching in secondary school

Young people usually go to secondary school at 11 years of age. By law, they must remain until they are 16, but some choose to stay on until they're 18. Those remaining in full-time education after 16 may continue at school, but sometimes go to either a sixth-form or further education college. Some colleges offer a traditional, academically based, sixth-form curriculum, and others a wider and, usually, more vocational range of courses.

Most young people attend state comprehensive schools. These cater for all levels of ability. There are also a number of schools that operate independently of the state system. These include the well-known 'public' schools that are normally governed by trusts. Comprehensive schools in England and Wales may have up to several thousand pupils and over a hundred staff. Independent schools, and comprehensive schools in Scotland, tend to be smaller and typically have 600-1,000 students.

Teachers in secondary schools usually specialise in one or two subjects and work with students of all ages and abilities within the school. As well as the kind of teaching duties already described, you may have to prepare assessments of coursework, write school reports, arrange visits to local employers and organise work experience for your students. You will also come into contact with parents, social workers, school governors and many other people in the community. Many independent and some state schools are residential during term time for pupils. These are known as boarding schools. In such a school you may have to live in and help to care for your students outside school hours.

Entry qualifications

As an arts or humanities graduate, to teach your subject in a state maintained school you need to follow your degree with a year's full-time training (or two years' part time) for the Postgraduate Certificate in Education (PGCE). Alternatively, you could follow the Registered Teacher Programme or the Graduate Teacher Programme. In each case your degree must be in a subject relevant to the National Curriculum. In addition to your degree you'll need at least a Grade C in GCSE English and Mathematics. And if you want to teach primary or middle school pupils, you'll also need a Grade C or above in a GCSE science subject. Your aim will be to achieve Qualified Teacher Status.

In Scotland you need a degree, including passes in two graduating courses in the subject you wish to teach, plus a Higher Grade or an equivalent in English and a Standard Grade (1–3) in mathematics.

From September 2006 those providing teacher training can charge you up to £3,000 per year in tuition fees. You won't have to pay anything up-front; your fees are simply added onto your student loan and are repaid when you are earning over £15,000. Trainee teachers will get some help with their fees as, in addition to the training bursary, a grant of up to £2,700 will be available from your LEA, of which £1,200 is not means-tested. You may also be eligible for further financial support from your training provider. Moreover, eligible trainees completing PGCE courses in England are entitled to receive a tax-free training bursary of £6,000-9,000, depending on the subject and course start date. Similar training bursaries are available in Wales, where eligible trainees receive £6,000-7,000, depending on their subject. Other incentives are currently also available for those completing their training.

The Scottish equivalent to the PGCE is the Postgraduate Diploma in Education (PGDE). This provides you with the Teaching Qualification in either Primary or Secondary Education. Once you have qualified, you must register with the General Teaching Council for Scotland before you can teach in a local education authority school. You then do a two-year probationary period as a teacher before you qualify for full registration.

You can get more information on funding for PGDE courses in Scotland from the Students Awards Agency for Scotland website, on www.student-support-saas.gov.uk/

You can also achieve Qualified Teacher Status while completing your first degree by following the Registered Teacher Programme (RTP). This is for people who have completed at least two years of higher education and can complete a degree while they train and work as a teacher. The programme normally takes two years and the school will need to work with a Higher Education Institution (HEI) that can provide a suitable 'top-up' degree programme.

The Graduate Teacher Programme (GTP) is for people who prefer to qualify while teaching. The programme lasts for up to one year, and you will be paid as an unqualified teacher during training in a school. You can complete the GTP in any English or Welsh maintained school, as long as they are prepared to employ you as an unqualified teacher for the duration of the programme. You can reply to an advertisement for the GTP programme, apply direct to a GTP provider, or find a job in a school as an unqualified teacher, provided they will support you throughout the programme.

Full details of entry into teaching in England and Wales is on the website of **The Training and Development Agency for Schools**, on www.tda.gov.uk, and in Scotland on the website of **Teaching in Scotland**, on www.teachinginscotland.com

Career development

Once you are a qualified teacher, opportunities for career development are good both within the classroom and in school administration. A couple of years in teaching are also good preparation for further training as an educational psychologist (although this training is changing, and holding teaching qualifications will no longer be essential for entry to educational psychology training).

Finding vacancies

You will start looking for your first teaching job while you are on your PGCE course. Many education authorities maintain close links with course providers. Alternatively, you can apply for advertised vacancies. These appear primarily in *The Times Educational Supplement, The Teacher* and *The Guardian*. Scottish vacancies will be found in *The Times Educational Supplement (Scotland), The Scotsman* and *The Herald*. Also look for vacancies on the internet.

Further information

You can get information on secondary school teaching in England and Wales from:

The Training and Development Agency for Schools
– Portland House, Bressenden Place, London SW1E 5TT.
Tel: 0870 4960 123. www.tda.gov.uk

In Scotland, information is available from:

Teaching in Scotland – Scottish Executive, Education Department, Area 2A Victoria Quay, Edinburgh EH6 6QQ. Tel: 0131 244 7930. www.teachinginscotland.com

Teaching in further education

This section looks at teaching in a wide range of colleges, adult education and other institutions. Some courses cover a broad range of academic as well as vocational subjects. Others specialise in areas such as agriculture, art and design, or hotel and catering work. Students can be of all ages, from 16- to 18-year-olds on full-time academic and vocational courses, to adults studying part time for vocational qualifications or pursuing their hobby interests through evening classes.

A lecturer's duties are similar to those of a secondary school teacher, especially when teaching academic subjects to the16-18 age group. However, with vocational subjects there is likely to be a stronger emphasis on practical work. Many part-time vocational courses are tied to the needs of local employers with whom lecturers have to maintain strong links.

Working conditions are similar to those for teachers in secondary schools, but paid holidays are shorter and lecturers usually have to work at least one evening session a week. Promotion prospects for those with a postgraduate teaching qualification are good.

Entry qualifications

Your degree must be relevant to the subject you wish to teach. You will also be required to have or work towards an appropriate teaching qualification, i.e. either a Postgraduate Certificate in Education (PGCE) specialising in FE/post-compulsory education, or a university Certificate in Education (Cert Ed). These qualifications give you the status of Qualified Teacher in Further Education (QTFE). Don't confuse this with Qualified Teacher Status (QTS) for which you need a PGCE for school teaching. If you have QTS you can work in FE, but if you have QTFE you cannot work as a qualified teacher in schools.

In Scotland, lecturers in further education need the Teaching Qualification (Further Education). There are four universities offering approved TQ(FE) courses – Aberdeen, Dundee, Stirling and Strathclyde.

Finding vacancies

Vacancies are advertised on the internet and in *The Times Educational Supplement, The Times Higher Educational Supplement, The Guardian,* and in Scotland, *The Herald* and *The Scotsman.*

Teaching in higher education

Teaching may be to either undergraduate or postgraduate students. Much of the teaching is through lectures that may be attended by more than 100 students. These may be supplemented by seminars with small groups of students and face-to-face tutorials with individuals. Seminars and tutorials involve interaction between teacher and students, with the students contributing their ideas and knowledge for discussion. Lecturers also supervise sessions of practical work, lead field trips and arrange work projects and placements.

Teaching at this level involves a lot of research and preparation. University teaching has to be at the forefront of knowledge, so it's vital that lecturers keep fully up to date with developments around the world in their specialist field. They must read extensively, and may attend seminars and conferences in other universities, sometimes overseas.

It also takes a great deal of time to set and mark assignments and examinations, carry out continuous assessment, and set up and monitor work projects and placements. Many lecturers also act as personal tutors to students, advising them on their studies, career aspirations, and personal problems. They often have a considerable administrative workload as well, which may include helping with student admissions, serving on committees and acting as external examiners for other institutions.

Teaching methods on degree courses have changed. Now there's more emphasis on helping students to take responsibility for their own learning and on developing the kinds of key skills that we looked at in Chapter four. Lecturers must give greater attention than before to the needs of individual students and help them to plan their own learning programmes.

Research is a vital function of any university. This is just as true for arts and humanities subjects as it is for science and technology. Universities are concerned not only with education but also with the advancement of knowledge. Moreover, much of the money supporting universities comes from research grants from government, industry, commerce and other external sources. The quality of research in every university department is assessed by the Higher Education Funding Council. The poorer the rating, the fewer funds the university attracts from the government and industry. Research is therefore often an important element in a lecturer's work, although the balance between teaching and research varies between posts and departments.

Although the academic (and teaching) year is only 30 weeks, staff do much of their research, administration and preparation for term time during the vacations. Many also work towards higher academic and professional qualifications, such as a PhD. In practice, many of them work hours at least as long as people in industry and commerce.

Entry qualifications

Competition for teaching posts in higher education is fierce, and more so in the arts and humanities than in science or technology. You'll need a good honours first degree in a relevant subject (a first or upper second) and will usually require a PhD or be working towards one. Until recently you needed no further qualification, but you are now normally required by universities to undertake formal postgraduate teaching training alongside doing the job. You can get more information of this accredited training from the Higher Education Academy (see below).

Career development

Many lecturers have little job security. They often work on short-term contracts of one, two or three years. These contracts have to be renewed if they are to keep their job. Promotion opportunities can be good but competition is intense. At present, career progress depends more on academic reputation than teaching ability. Publication of original research in learned journals and books, a PhD and administrative skills are often important prerequisites for advancement. Those who become recognised as experts often earn extra money, and add to their reputations, through outside work. This can include consultancy, writing, broadcasting and speaking at conferences.

Finding vacancies

Vacancies are advertised in *The Guardian, The Times Higher Educational Supplement, The Independent* and other 'quality' newspapers. Vacancies are also advertised on the The Association of University Teachers' website (see below).

Further information

More details on teaching in further and higher education are available from:

The Association of University Teachers – Egmont House, 25-31 Tavistock Place, London WC1H 9UT. Tel: 020 7670 9700. www.aut.org.uk

The Higher Education Academy – Innovation Way, York Science Park, Heslington, York YO10 5BR. Tel: 01904 717500. www.heacademy.ac.uk

The University and College Lecturers' Union – 27 Britannia Street, London WC1X 9JP. Tel: 020 7837 3636. www.natfhe.org.uk

Chapter six
Careers using English

All employers value the ability to use English accurately and persuasively, in speech and in writing. However, there are several careers where the skilful use of English is the main qualification. The chief ones are book publishing (especially editorial work) and journalism (press and broadcasting). This chapter looks at each of these.

Other careers that can make very good use of your oral communication skills are public relations, sales and advertising. Contrary to popular belief, you don't need to be an extrovert to sell, and many areas of selling need good intelligence and an analytical mind. You will find information on public relations, sales and advertising in Chapter seven.

Book publishing

Some people have predicted that electronic media will replace book publishing. But the UK book publishing industry produced some 160,000 new titles in 2004 – 30,000 more than in the year before. This suggests that any forecast of the extinction of books was somewhat premature. However, electronic publishing is growing rapidly and many publishers are already actively involved, and a handful of authors have experimented with publishing directly onto the internet.

According to the Publishers Association (www.publishers.org.uk) there are 60,000 active publishers in the UK, although this includes a number of imprints. The number registered for VAT was 2,275 in 2002/3. They had total sales of £3,053.5 million. Books aimed at the general public account for almost two-thirds of the industry.

The main functions in book publishing, apart from writing the books, are:

- editorial

- design and production

- marketing (including sales, public relations and publicity)

- distribution

- contracts and rights

- administration (including accounts and computing).

We will concentrate here on the editorial function, as this is the area where your English degree is likely to be most relevant. Publishing is one of the top preferences for arts and humanities graduates, with editorial the most popular function. However, editorial offers the fewest opportunities in book publishing, because it employs only one in five of the people in book publishing. Consequently, competition for places is very high.

Some of the other functions offer a somewhat easier way to start in the publishing industry (with the possibility of moving into editorial work later), and are looked at briefly.

'There are three difficulties in authorship: to write anything worth publishing, to find honest men to publish it, and to get sensible men to read it.'

The Reverend Charles C Colton, British author and clergyman

Commissioning editors

Commissioning editors find new books to publish. Editors sometimes decide to publish a book because of its literary merit, even though it may only appeal to a minority of people. But publishing is a business like any other and must make profits to survive. It is the role of the commissioning editor to know what will sell in their market and to obtain manuscripts accordingly. Commissioning editors need to be widely read and to have an instinct for what readers want.

'If you want to get rich from writing, write the sort of thing that's read by persons who move their lips when they're reading to themselves.'

Don Marquis, American writer and columnist

The manuscripts of unpublished books are usually sent to publishers by literary agents acting on behalf of authors. The agents use their experience to match manuscripts to publishers, so that a thriller is not sent to a publisher specialising in cookery books, or a reference book to a fiction house. Authors also send in unsolicited manuscripts themselves, but less than one in fifty of these get published. Commissioning editors decide which manuscripts to accept or reject.

Many publishers, particularly of technical or educational books, specifically order or 'commission' books to be written. Once a need for a work on a particular subject has been identified, the commissioning editor will find an expert or experts to write it. The commissioning editor will agree the contents of the manuscript, and when it must be delivered, with the author. The editor will also negotiate the clauses of the contract with the author and oversee the production of the book from editing through to typesetting (now usually replaced by computer setting at the publishers) – although this latter role may be undertaken by a managing editor. A production controller will liaise with the setter, and oversee the printing and binding.

Copy-editors

Supporting the work of commissioning editors (and managing editors) are copy-editors (text is called 'copy') or desk-editors. Their function is to read the manuscript and prepare it for setting. They check manuscripts for logical structure, accuracy, clarity and the effective use of language. They cut repetitive statements and contradictions and correct errors of spelling, grammar and punctuation. Extensive revisions are sometimes needed. All these must be discussed and agreed with the author. Writing is lonely, difficult and often frustrating and authors sometimes vent their frustrations on their editors. Editors must be good with people if they are to get the best out of their writers.

'I get a lot of letters from people. They say 'I want to be a writer. What should I do?' I tell them to stop writing to me and to get on with it.'

Ruth Rendell, English crime novelist

Once edited, copy goes to design and production to be turned into a printed book. Illustrations may be chosen or commissioned, involving discussion between the author, artist and editor. Note that computers are now used by all publishers, in almost every department, including editorial. Most authors use word-processing packages on their personal computers and are almost always expected to supply their manuscripts on floppy disk or as an email attachment. The edited text is usually sent to the typesetter on disk. An editor will, therefore, often work on screen: it is important to have good word-processing skills. There is an increasing move towards using freelance staff in publishing. Freelance copy-editors usually move into such work after several years' experience within a publishing house.

Other functions

Experience of other functions makes good preparation for an editorial career. Jobs in marketing or rights are especially useful. Working in these areas will develop an awareness of what is required of a book if it is going to sell. You will also be in contact with authors.

Marketing

This area covers all the activities necessary to promote and sell books. Publicity staff produce advertising, press releases, book lists and other materials. They also run special events such as lecture tours and arrange appearances by authors on TV and radio chat shows to promote their latest book. Sales staff sell the books to the wholesale and retail book trade, to specialist library suppliers, or direct to end customers such as schools or colleges. Marketing employs more people than editorial and production combined.

'The covers of this book are too far apart.'

Book review by Ambrose Bierce, American journalist

Contracts and rights

Staff in this department handle the legal side of publishing. They cover the initial agreements and contracts with authors and any issues arising from further developments of a book, such as translation or the sale of film or serial rights.

Entry qualifications

It's very hard to go directly into editorial work because there are so many applicants for each opening. You'll need a good knowledge of English grammar, punctuation and the precise meanings of words. You must be widely read and be able to demonstrate a genuine interest in books. If you hope to join a publisher in such specialist fields as science, medicine or art history, you will need an interest in and some knowledge of the field. You also need to have a meticulous eye for detail and be well organised. You must be good with people, not only authors, but others in the publishing team. You must also be adaptable and willing to 'muck-in' with the most mundane jobs, such as photocopying manuscripts. A modern foreign language is required in some international publishing houses. As in any highly competitive job market, a postgraduate qualification can be helpful – in this case a postgraduate degree or diploma in publishing.

Your career may start in copy-editing. Alternatively, many graduates join a publishing house in any job they can get, and then apply for an editorial vacancy when one arises. Another option is to join a small publisher, where people take on a range of general duties including some editorial work.

Training and career development

Only the largest publishers offer formal training. However, there is a variety of courses which you can undertake once you have started work. The leading course provider is the Publishing Training Centre.

Career development for editorial staff is fairly restricted. Becoming a commissioning editor is the pinnacle of editorial achievement. However, if you can get some experience in other functions, or show real commercial awareness while you are in editorial, you may find opportunities to move into general management. Don't join publishing for money – the industry in general is badly paid. Your chief reward is the satisfaction of nursing new books into print.

Finding vacancies

Final-year students should check with their careers services, consult the main graduate careers directories – *Graduate Employment and Training* (known as GET) (published by Hobsons) and *Prospects Directory* (published by Prospects), and search the internet. General publishing vacancies may be advertised in *The Guardian* (Mondays and Saturdays), *The Independent* (Wednesdays), *The Times* and *The Daily Telegraph* (Thursdays). The two main trade magazines to check, both weeklies, are *The Bookseller* and *Publishing News*.

Further information

The Publishing Training Centre – Book House, 45 East Hill, Wandsworth, London SE18 2QZ. Tel: 020 8874 2718. www.train4publishing.co.uk

Journalism

'Literature is the art of writing something that will be read twice; journalism, what will be grasped at once.'

Cyril Connolly, English critic and editor

Journalists collect and disseminate information. They keep the public informed about news and current affairs, but are rarely held in high public esteem. Although the modern tabloid press is often blamed for this dislike and distrust, it's not new. A hundred years ago Henrik Ibsen said:

'It is inexcusable for scientists to torture animals; let them make their experiments on journalists and politicians.'

Henrik Ibsen, Norwegian dramatist

Working as a journalist

Work is available in two main areas: broadcasting and the press. The press can be further subdivided into press (or news) agencies, and newspapers and periodicals.

Broadcasting

This used to be the exclusive domain of the BBC. Now with international, national and local commercial radio and television stations there are many more opportunities than in the past. The BBC now expects its journalists to train in both TV and radio, while most of those in the commercial stations work in either one or the other. Apart from gathering stories and writing copy, they may also act as presenters and operate studio equipment. Some also work as researchers on documentary programmes.

News (or press) agencies

These agencies feed news to other media. The most famous news agencies are the Press Association and Reuters. Agencies provide objective information for other journalists to use. (There have been notable exceptions to this; some state-controlled press agencies overseas have sometimes been used as propaganda organisations.) The work of news agencies is especially useful in those situations where other media representatives may not be present. This might include war zones where journalists from specific countries have been excluded for political reasons.

The UK press

The press is made up of 125 daily and Sunday newspapers, about 800 weekly newspapers and some 1000 weekly local free papers ('free sheets'). There are also around 1700 consumer magazines and 4000 trade and technical periodicals (magazines or journals issued at regular intervals, normally weekly, monthly or quarterly).

It's probably worth checking out the annual *Willings Press Guide* that can be found in most reference libraries (Volume 1 covers the UK) or consult the *British Rate and Data (BRAD)* website through your university library. These list every magazine (be it consumer and special interest, or business and professional) published in Britain. Each entry gives information on the publisher, address, telephone, fax numbers, website, frequency of publication and, on some occasions, a brief editorial profile.

Many new titles are born each month, while others die. In news agency and broadcasting work speed is essential; audiences expect news to be constantly updated. Newspapers can't compete with radio and TV for speed, so they offer more detailed news and analysis. Journalists can develop as specialist reporters or 'correspondents'. National papers have journalists who specialise in one subject. On other papers, and in news agencies, they usually mix general reporting with one or more specialisms. The main specialist areas are:

- agriculture
- broadcasting

- business (industry and commerce)
- education
- entertainment (film, theatre, music)
- fashion
- finance (including the City)
- food and drink
- foreign news
- home interests
- holidays and travel
- motoring
- political (local or national) and parliamentary affairs
- science and technology
- social affairs
- sport
- women's issues.

Entry qualifications

You don't need any qualifications to enter journalism other than your degree. However, competition for places is tough, and a postgraduate qualification in journalism will give you an advantage. You must be able to write factual, concise and clear English. The emphasis in journalism is on accuracy, clarity, brevity and speed. An interest in current affairs and a good general knowledge are essential. You need curiosity. You must combine tact and sensitivity with assertiveness; you will have to interview people of all kinds, some of whom won't want to talk to you. Having physical and mental stamina is important, because the job can involve a lot of travel and irregular hours. Reporters in newspapers, radio and TV often work evenings and weekends; shift working is common on daily newspapers and in broadcasting.

Almost all journalists today key their stories directly into computers; so basic word-processing skills are essential. To be a radio or television journalist you also need a good speaking voice. When submitting a job application, you may have to complete a tape as well as an application form. To enter periodical publishing it is also helpful if you have a good knowledge of the subject covered by the magazine you want to join.

Experience on a student or community publication is valuable. It is also useful to have had a brief work experience placement on a newspaper. It is also worth writing to some local newspaper editors asking if you can join their team of reporters as an unpaid observer for a day or two.

Training

A number of training routes are described below.

Trainee reporter

Almost every journalist starts as a trainee reporter, usually on a regional daily or local weekly newspaper. They cover everything: local council meetings and court cases, fires and floods, accidents, political demonstrations, sports events and interviews with visiting celebrities.

If you have been recruited into the industry from school or university, you will be regarded as a 'direct entrant'. Most companies will expect you to enter into a two-year training contract during which time you will receive basic training. Most companies will register you with the National Council for the Training of Journalists (NCTJ) and provide you with a distance-learning foundation course to study. After about six months you should ideally attend a block-release or day-release course at college, during which time you will sit the NCTJ's preliminary series of examinations. Following a further period of employment, you will have the opportunity to obtain the NCTJ's National Certificate or a National (Scottish) Vocational Qualification at Level 4.

Postgraduate course in journalism

If you attend a postgraduate course in journalism accredited by the NCTJ prior to taking up a post (known as 'pre-entry'), you'll serve a three-month probationary period before entering a training contract. The length of your training period may be reduced to reflect the experience you gained during your postgraduate course. Postgraduate courses recognised by the NCTJ can be found on the NCJT website (see below). There are also 'Fast Track' postgraduate courses lasting from 18 to 20 weeks. These too can be found on the NCJT website.

Postgraduate courses that are not accredited by the NCTJ have little credibility in the industry.

Magazine journalism

Training in magazine journalism is less formal than in newspapers. Many graduates enter in junior positions and receive training that varies from informal learning from others while on the job, through to a structured programme of development. However, there are three new courses that are accredited by the NCTJ for graduates wishing to enter the magazine industry. These are at Harlow College, Brighton College and Liverpool Community College. These last from 19-20 weeks.

The Periodical Training Council also offers a wide range of short courses (half-day to two days). These are listed on the PPA website (see below).

Broadcast journalism

All the main employers in broadcast journalism – including the BBC, ITV and Sky – support the Broadcast Journalism Training Council (BJTC). The Council also accredits courses in 18 colleges and universities. Most radio and TV journalists now start on local radio before progressing through regional and national radio to TV. Consequently, most courses approved by the Council concentrate on radio and online journalism, although giving some coverage to television. Most, but not all, BJTC recognised courses are full-time postgraduate courses lasting a year. Look up the BJTC website (www. bjtc.org.uk) for an up-to-date list of these courses.

Career development

In newspapers there is no set career structure. You may for a time head specialist parts of the paper, such as City or women's pages. You may become a news editor, allocating stories to individual reporters and attending editorial conferences. You may become a sub-editor. As a sub-editor you'd work on stories fed in by reporters, often rewriting opening paragraphs, cutting for length and giving stories an angle. You'd also write the headlines.

If you want to reach senior posts (such as deputy editor and editor) where you have control over the content of a whole publication, you'll need to have been a sub-editor and probably have headed a number of specialist sections.

Companies that produce magazines vary in their organisational structure according to their size. The three most common job titles you will come across are assistant editor (normally a junior level of journalist), deputy editor (the number two, who both writes and does much of the sub-editing) and editor (in overall charge of the content).

Finding vacancies

Most newspapers get plenty of applicants without needing to advertise, but many still advertise vacancies in their own appointments pages. Most nationally advertised vacancies appear in *The Guardian* on Mondays and Saturdays, and the weekly *UK Press Gazette*. Details of BBC training schemes can be found in the BBC graduate recruitment brochure, which you can get from your careers service or on their website (see below).

Further information

National Council for the Training of Journalists – Latton Bush Centre, Southern Way, Harlow, Essex CM18 7BL. Tel: 01279 430009. www.nctj.com

Periodicals Training Council – Queen's House, 55-56 Lincoln's Inn Fields, London WC2A 3LJ. Tel: 020 7404 4168. www.ppa.co.uk

Scottish Newspaper Publishers Association – 48 Palmerston Place, Edinburgh EH12 5DE. Tel: 0131 220 4353. www.snpa.org.uk

BBC – PO Box 7000, London W5 2WY. Tel: 020 8752 5252. www.bbc.co.uk

Broadcast Journalism Training Council – 39 Westbourne Gardens, London W2 5NR. Tel: 020 7727 9522. www.bjtc.org.uk

Chapter seven
Careers using communication and media

You'll find that some of the careers that can make use of communication and media studies overlap with careers using English – such as press and broadcast journalism. Consequently, it is recommended that you read Chapters six and seven together.

This chapter looks at public relations (PR), sales and advertising. As in the last chapter, all these employers put a high value on your ability to communicate effectively by the use of accurate and persuasive English, both in speech and in writing. But the greater understanding of people's psychology that you should have acquired on a communication or media studies course should be an additional strength.

Public relations

The aim of public relations is to manage the reputation and image of an organisation or, sometimes, an individual. The job focuses on developing and maintaining good relationships with everyone whose support and goodwill are essential to the client's success. These may include customers and potential customers, suppliers, journalists, shareholders, trading partners, employees and potential employees, the stock market, community leaders, environmentalists and government at all levels.

Public relations specialists are used by all kinds of people and organisations: commercial and industrial firms, central and local government, universities, celebrities, charities, politicians, public services, trade and professional bodies and environmental and other pressure groups. Some organisations have their own public relations (or public affairs) departments; others use PR agencies that act on their behalf. More than half work in the PR departments of their own organisations, and the Government is the largest single employer.

Public relations staff provide stories about their client or organisation and its products where appropriate. These stories have to have 'news value' if they are going to be used by the media – so finding new and novel angles is a major challenge. The information also has to be carefully targeted. Customers will be interested in new product launches; shareholders and the stock market want news of the financial health of the business; environmentalists will want to know about the development of a cleaner manufacturing process, raw materials from sustainable sources, and so on. Most of the information is issued through press releases, press conferences, brochures, the annual report and house magazines. Your work will bring you into close contact with journalists. Feature articles may be placed in the media. You might even 'ghost write' speeches and articles for a client's executives.

An important aspect of PR work is crisis management. When something goes wrong, or when an organisation does something that might be unpopular, PR people have to put the best possible light on it and minimise any damage to the organisation's reputation. Sometimes this can be planned in advance, such as when an organisation makes people redundant, puts its prices up or builds a factory in a beauty spot. On other occasions problems are totally unexpected, such as the accidental release of a pollutant into the environment, the arrest of a senior executive on criminal charges or the failure of a company product leading to the death of a customer. Often the first you may know about the crisis is a call from the media wanting an instant reaction and 'a quote'.

The aim of PR is to project an 'image' of the organisation. This can extend to the design of a 'house style' for the headed paper and other stationery, the livery of the organisation's vehicles, product packaging, and so on. Some agencies specialise in this area of design.

Other agencies specialise in producing annual reports, brochures, and videos and films. These are often called 'corporate communications' consultancies. All these activities are part of the PR business. However, PR is generally distinct from advertising.

As you can see, PR work is varied. The range of your duties will depend on where you work. In-house departments vary in the scope of their activities: they may divide their work between internal staff and external experts. Some agencies specialise in one area of PR work, such as corporate communications. Others handle all aspects of PR. However, typically your work will include going to client briefings and other meetings, making presentations, attending press conferences and writing material for public or press information.

Entry qualifications

There are no preconditions for membership, although 95% of new entrants to the Chartered Institute of Public Relations (CIPR), the professional body for PR, are now graduates. Quite a few new entrants to the profession transfer from journalism.

You must be articulate and able to write clearly and succinctly. Assertiveness, but not aggression, is essential. You'll need a lot of self-confidence to handle tough questions from a hostile journalist, to give a speech, to cope with a dissatisfied customer or to talk to a visiting celebrity. Obviously, you have to remain calm under pressure.

Training and career development

There are postgraduate degree courses in PR that are approved by the CIPR. These are offered by the University of the Arts, London; Bournemouth University; Central Lancashire University; The Dublin Institute of Technology; Leeds Metropolitan University; London Metropolitan University; Manchester Metropolitan University; Queen Margaret University College, Edinburgh; University of Stirling; Trinity and All Souls University College, University of Leeds; the University of Wales in Cardiff; and West Herts College. However, a relevant first or higher degree isn't essential, although a relevant postgraduate degree does improve your chances of employment in a fiercely competitive marketplace.

Training is normally on the job, working with a senior account executive. The CIPR runs distance-learning courses leading to the Institute's Advanced Certificate and to the Diploma.

Job titles vary a lot. You may work your way up in a large consultancy from account executive through senior account executive to a partnership. In the Government Information Service you will be known as an 'information officer'; there are various grades through which you can progress (see the information about working in public service in Chapter fifteen).

Finding vacancies

The CIPR runs a 'PR Jobshop' on its website listing current job vacancies. You will also find PR vacancies advertised in the magazine *PR Week* and also on its website at www.prweekjobs.com

Also look out for opportunities with those organisations that have their own public affairs or public relations departments. Consult the main graduate recruitment directories such as *Graduate Employment and Training (GET)* and *Prospects Directory* (see Chapter twenty-two, for details) to find out where there are graduate openings.

Further information

Chartered Institute of Public Relations – PR Centre, 32 St James's Square, London SW1Y 4JR. Tel: 020 7766 3333. www.cipr.co.uk

Sales

'Everyone lives by selling something.'

Robert Louis Stevenson, Scottish novelist and poet

Although few of us are initially attracted to a career in sales, most of us do enjoy persuading others to accept our point of view. Whether this involves a subtle academic point or a decision on how to spend the evening, we tend to be pleased if we convince others to see or do things our way. The art of persuasion isn't just a useful social skill. It's also invaluable in any career. Most jobs involve team working. You need to be persuasive if you are to:

- persuade subordinates to give you their willing effort
- obtain the help of colleagues over whom you've no authority
- win the support of your boss for any initiatives you want to take
- get good service from your suppliers
- persuade customers to buy from you.

Many areas of selling require good intelligence and an analytical mind. Yet mention 'selling' to people and they visualise a glib extrovert pressurising the unwilling into buying the unwanted. In the past, there was some truth in this stereotype. Businesses were geared to production and their sales staff had to sell whatever the company chose to make.

Now, most businesses have a better understanding of their customers' needs. They are 'market-led', creating products and services for which they've identified a clear need. Also, customers have become more knowledgeable – they are more aware of the choices open to them and have higher expectations of both the products and the quality of service that they get from suppliers.

'Any fool can paint a picture, but it takes a wise man to be able to sell it.'

Samuel Butler, English novelist and satirist

Because winning and looking after customers are central to the survival of every business, selling is a key function. Selling ranges from trading on market stalls through to negotiating the sale of aircraft to governments and airlines. However, graduate sales careers rarely involve selling directly to the public, the only major exception being the sale of financial services.

There are two basic types of selling, canvassing and servicing, although both are often combined in one job. Canvassing is approaching potential customers for the first time to win an initial order. Servicing is following up earlier sales and obtaining new orders from existing customers.

The principles of selling are similar whatever the product. You have to identify a customer's needs through intelligent questions and discussion. You can't sell anything until the customer recognises a need. You must then describe, briefly and persuasively, how your product will satisfy that need better than competing products, and provide convincing evidence to support your claims. If the customer raises objections, and most will, you must overcome them without entering an argument.

'Win the argument and lose the sale.'

Old sales proverb

You will need to negotiate prices and delivery dates. You will have to liaise with your own production and delivery departments in order to meet the delivery schedules. And you'll have to make follow-up calls to ensure that the customer is satisfied, to answer any queries or resolve any complaints, and to ask for more orders.

Selling can be either face to face 'field sales', or by telephone. If you are selling on the telephone you could be working in a call centre and making 30-40 calls a day. Working in field sales, you may call on several hundred customers every few weeks, or visit 20 or so a week, or even fewer depending on the nature of the business. A salesperson selling a technical product to a really large user – such as industrial paints to a car manufacturer – may be fully occupied in caring for the needs of that one customer. It is increasingly common for field sales staff to keep in touch with their office by mobile phone and laptop computer.

Entry qualifications

You seldom need any formal qualifications except in areas of technical selling where you may need a relevant degree. What you will need is a questioning and analytical mind to discuss and identify customer needs and to relate these to your products. You also need the social skills and maturity to develop relationships with people of all ages and at all levels of seniority.

You must be articulate so that you can present and defend a cogent argument clearly and persuasively. You must also be a good listener. You must be able to write clearly so you can correspond with your customers, supply reports to management, and provide clear briefings to your marketing, production and despatch departments. In field sales your work is less closely supervised than in a call centre, so you do need to be self-reliant and a good organiser of your own work and travel schedules.

Training

Companies differ enormously in the quality of training they provide. Make sure you join a company with a structured training programme that is not limited to basic knowledge of the product and a few days shadowing an existing salesperson.

Career development

In field sales you typically move from salesperson to field sales manager or area sales manager (in telephone selling the equivalent may be a telephone trainer), then on to deputy sales manager, sales manager and sales director. The qualities needed in sales management are different from those needed in selling. You will probably be responsible for managing a team of salespeople, and may not do any direct selling yourself. Some people prefer the independence of remaining in the field. They may develop a portfolio of major customers. These people can sometimes earn more than anybody else in the company.

Finding vacancies

Newly qualified graduates are probably best consulting the major graduate careers directories (and their websites) – *Graduate Employment and Training (GET)* and *Prospects Directory* (see Chapter twenty-two for details). You will also find many sales posts advertised on the major recruitment websites such as Monster, Fish4Jobs and CareerJet. Sales vacancies are also advertised in all the major broadsheet newspapers – especially *The Daily Telegraph* (Thursdays) and *The Sunday Times*.

Some employers, mostly in financial services, recruit people to sell on commission only. You should not even consider this until you have had considerable sales experience and have some cash savings to fall back on if things go wrong.

Advertising

Advertising is not as modern an industry as you might think. The first known advertisement was found on a 3,000-year-old papyrus in the ruins of Thebes. This offered a reward for the return of a runaway slave to 'the shop of Hapu the weaver, where the best cloth is woven to your desires...' That last phrase suggests that even then the art of advertising copywriting wasn't new.

'The trade in advertising is now so near to perfection that it is not easy to propose any improvement.'

Dr Samuel Johnson, writer and lexicographer, in
The Idler, **1759**

There are three jobs in advertising that you might consider: working as an account executive, working in a media department or agency, and copywriting.

Working as an account executive

An account executive looks after a group of clients in an advertising agency and is in almost daily contact with them. As an account executive, you are the link between the agency and the client. You must get the best possible work, on behalf of your client, from your colleagues in other departments and your suppliers – copywriters, art directors, media executives, researchers and administrators.

An account executive has a glamorous image, and many people are attracted by the travel and entertainment that the work often entails. But the novelty of rising at dawn to catch an early train or plane and getting home late in the evening soon wears thin – especially if you're doing it two or three times a week. Even lunching a client in an expensive restaurant loses its glamour when, in mid-mouthful, you are asked to explain why the client's sales are falling, or why the production costs for a new television commercial have gone over budget.

The account executive's job is to keep clients happy. If the agency loses a big client, the account executive responsible is often dismissed. It's a very stressful job. The late David Ogilvie, who built Ogilvie & Mather into the world's fourth largest advertising agency, said the head of an agency 'must be a good leader of frightened people'. He also quoted a study that showed that the death rate from stress-related causes was 14% higher among senior advertising executives than their counterparts in other white-collar occupations. However, you'll certainly be offered plenty of intellectual and management challenges. Being an account executive is also one of the best routes to top management in advertising.

If you aim to develop your long-term career in advertising, ask your employer to sponsor you either on the Communication, Advertising and Marketing Education Foundation (CAM) Certificate and Diploma, or the programme of residential courses run by the Institute of Practitioners in Advertising (IPA). Some agencies prefer the CAM scheme; some, the IPA.

Matthew Styant

Matthew, 27, describes his career progress which has led him to working in a senior role in an advertising agency.

Career profile

Job title: senior account manager

Employer: MediaCom

A Levels: French, geography, economics

Degree: BA modern European studies with French

University: University College London.

'I chose my A level subjects because they were the ones I enjoyed. At the time I had absolutely no idea what degree I was going to do. I only applied once I'd actually got my A level grades. I chose European studies with French, a four-year course, because I wanted to spend a year living in another culture and another country just to see what it would be like.

One of the great things about the course was that it consisted of many parts. There were about 30 of us reading the subject, but we all did different modules. You could specialise in things like European politics, European geography or social philosophy. You do a huge number of different modules in your first year. Depending on those you prefer, you narrow your choice in subsequent years and study more specialist areas. I specialised in geography. As French was my major subject, this was the geography of France. In my final year I also took a course in French cinema.

The language part of the course was quite intensive before going to France. I chose to spend a year studying geography at the University of Grenoble. And I managed to squeeze in a bit of skiing as well.

In the summer before I went to France my mind turned to what I should do after graduation. I started eliminating those careers that I didn't want to do. I didn't fancy accountancy or a law conversion course. But it wasn't until halfway through my final year that I contacted an old school friend who happened to work at MediaCom. He suggested I come and get some work experience in a media agency and see if I enjoyed it.

I did a couple of weeks' donkey work, but saw the inside workings of an advertising media agency. I really enjoyed and liked what I saw, and pretty much made up my mind that it was a career that excited me and something I wanted to do. I liked the relaxed atmosphere and the general buzz about the place. The people were passionate and excited about the advertising campaigns that they were running.

I still wasn't a 100% sure that I would go into advertising. And, in fact, I didn't start at MediaCom until about 18 months after graduation. In between I worked as a cycle tour guide in France. I did that for two summers, and spent my winters looking for jobs and sending off application forms.

When I applied to MediaCom they interviewed me for a couple of positions. There are many different departments in an advertising agency. The one that seemed to fit my skill-set best was in outdoor advertising, planning and buying campaigns on billboards, posters, buses and so on.

Since joining I have had one double promotion in March this year. This took me from an outdoor media planner, bypassing account manager, to a senior account manager. On a day-to-day basis I liaise directly with clients and the media planners here. I will receive a brief – with an idea of strategy, budget and target audience and so on – and it is up to me to come up with an integrated outdoor campaign that best fits the brief. Another part of my job is to work with the creative agencies. I also get involved in new business presentations – very exciting and a lot of fun – but it can mean very long hours. Many times I've been in the office until ten at night.

My university studies have helped my career substantially. It was not what I learned about France and social history and philosophy, but more the skills I learned in things like meeting deadlines, networking and analysis skills.

I would thoroughly recommend doing an arts or humanities degree to anyone thinking about it. It is far more general than a science or law degree. But the skills you get from an arts or humanities degree are things that you can transfer to almost any walk of life and almost any career. You'll find the experience you gain helps you to deal with deadlines, the volume of reading and so on, and makes you responsible for looking after your own work – something you don't get at school.'

Working in a media department or agency

In the past each agency had its own media department. This would recommend the best medium, or mix of media, in which to place a particular advertisement or advertising campaign, and then buy the space or time on behalf of the client. But in recent years many media departments have become independent media agencies. Today there appears to be a move back to agency-owned media departments. So media executives may be employed in either, although doing the same basic job.

As a media executive you have to weigh up the respective merits of different newspapers, periodicals, radio and television stations, cinema, poster sites, websites and so on, in terms of their potential to reach the client's 'target audience'. You'll draw on circulation figures; readership, listening and viewing surveys; and many other statistical sources.

You need an analytical mind and the ability to express the statistical data in lay terms. You also buy 'time' or 'space' from media owners. Advertising rates are often open to discussion, especially if you are buying in volume, so you should also have a taste for negotiation. Graduates are often found on the other side, selling advertising space or time on behalf of media owners. Much of this is done via the telephone direct to advertisers. However, with large advertisers and with agencies the selling is usually carried out face to face.

Copywriting

Copywriters are employed in advertising agencies to write advertising, TV and radio commercials and other promotional materials for clients. Some are also used by corporate communications companies to write brochures and annual reports. It is probably the most disciplined form of writing after poetry.

Many advertising agency copywriters have become well-known authors. They include Dorothy L Sayers, Aldous Huxley, Salman Rushdie, Jack Rosenthal, Fay Weldon, Len Deighton and James Herbert. James White set up the world's first advertising agency in London in 1800, with Charles Lamb, the essayist, as his copywriter.

'It is easier to write ten passably effective sonnets than one effective advertisement.'

Aldous Huxley, English novelist and former copywriter

Copywriting is extremely hard to enter. This is because identifying an individual's talent is difficult until it's been tested on the job. However, good copywriters are rare so, once established, the best can ask their own price. To write good copy, you must understand the characteristics of the product and what will motivate your audience to buy it. You need imagination to find new ways of saying things that have been said scores of times before, and to catch and hold the public's interest. And you should be aware of prevailing fashions in order to keep your ideas one step ahead of the trend.

You must work well with other people, especially clients, creative directors and designers. Much of your copy will be dissected by others, changed and often rejected. Many clients are very conservative and reluctant to accept new ideas. You need the temperament to accept this without anger or frustration. Copywriters for TV commercials tend to be specialists who can think in visual terms and work closely with a producer. Brochure writers too are often specialists.

Entry qualifications

Copywriting doesn't need any formal qualifications, although it is normal to have a degree. You will need to be a fluent, imaginative and disciplined writer. You need to understand people and their motivations and you must have an interest in helping businesses to achieve commercial success. You'll need to be a good team worker able to work to tight deadlines and have a high tolerance to frustration.

Many copywriting entrants have worked in journalism, marketing or sales. Otherwise you probably need some relevant training. Advertising writing or creative advertising courses are run at several universities and colleges.

Before you apply for any copywriting posts, study the press advertisements and film, TV, internet and radio commercials around you. Read and view them critically. Who do they address? What's the key message? What motives are they appealing to? How could the advertisements be improved? Write your own versions. Prepare a portfolio of advertisements you've written to show creative directors at interview. And when applying for a job as a copywriter, remember that any CV and application letter is an advertisement aimed at *your* target audience.

Training and career development

Advertising agencies don't have trainee schemes for copywriters. You learn on the job. Your progress as a copywriter will depend on the success of the campaigns you work on. This will be reflected in your salary and your reputation in the industry. Career development is often achieved by moving between agencies. (Note that job titles are often designed to impress clients rather than to indicate your real status – e.g. designers are almost always called 'art directors'.) The best copywriters are very highly paid. Some, like David Ogilvie, Charles Saatchi, Raymond Rubicam and Leo Burnett, end up heading international advertising groups. Some TV commercial and video scriptwriters move into working on feature films.

Finding vacancies

You should read the job advertisements in *Campaign, Marketing, Marketing Week* and *Media Week*. These publications also give news of agencies winning new business and of staff changes, so offering you clues as to which agencies may be seeking new writers. It is also worth getting hold of the *Campaign Career Guide* (see www.brandrepublic. com/magazines/campaign). Also check the internet websites (and also the IPA website – see below) as well as the quality press – especially *The Guardian*.

A speculative application to someone you'd like to work for, if you've researched the agency thoroughly, can win you an interview. Your letter will need to be original and totally convincing – not just novel for the sake of novelty. Even if the creative director can't offer you a job, you may get some good advice and even some introductions to other agencies.

Further information

CAM Education Foundation – Moor Hall, Cookham, Maidenhead SL6 9QH. Tel: 01628 427180. www.camfoundation.com

Institute of Practitioners in Advertising – 44 Belgrave Square, London SW1X 8QS. Tel: 020 7235 7020. www.ipa.co.uk

Chapter eight
Careers using librarianship and related subjects

We live in an age of information – so much of it that someone described it as the age of information pollution. It has been calculated that the sum of human knowledge now doubles every 18 months. Keeping abreast of this torrent of information is the huge task of librarians and other information workers. And not only must they look after paper-based material, there are also film, video, photographic, microfiche, audio, CD-ROM and other electronic records.

Library or information work

When we think of a librarian we think of someone who looks after shelves and shelves of dusty books or manuscripts and lends these out to borrowers. This isn't a real reflection of the job – which should be more realistically thought of as information management.

In Britain alone we create huge masses of information. We publish around 160,000 new books a year, 125 daily newspapers, several hundred weekly papers, and thousands of weekly, monthly and quarterly periodicals. In addition, there are theses produced by academic researchers, policy documents and records produced by every government department and agency, papers produced by businesses, and much more.

This material must be managed in such a way that data can be retrieved when needed. Some records have only a short useful life and can be scrapped quickly. Many must be kept for years for legal, administrative and other purposes. Some are of historical significance and must be retained in permanent archives. As you will see from the profile of Jennie Hood (page 132), the Freedom of Information Act has meant that many public records that were 'filed and forgotten' are now being properly catalogued and made available to the public on request.

The work of librarians and information specialists is very similar. The work involves the storage, classification and indexing of records. With many types of material you could be involved in deciding what needs to be kept for historical, legal, financial and other reasons, and what can be disposed of. You would need to ensure that anyone authorised to do so can easily access the collection. And you would have to handle internal and external requests for information.

Librarians in public libraries are responsible for the selection, purchase, cataloguing and arrangement of books, periodicals, videos, CDs, information packs and other materials. Some run special services such as mobile libraries, children's activities and business sections. Librarians also answer queries from the public. Most if not all public libraries now have computer terminals for the public to access the internet, undertake training programmes and so on. Consequently, librarians have to be familiar with computers so they can assist users.

Academic librarians serve both staff and students. In collaboration with their academic colleagues, they select materials to support the study and research taking place in the institution. Much time is spent showing students how to make the most of the facilities available (such as the computerised catalogue, the internet, etc). Many academic librarians specialise in a particular subject area.

Librarians and information specialists also work in research organisations, professional institutions, local and national government and other bodies. They usually manage specialist collections in a particular area of government, industry or field of science or technology. Some may manage libraries in large companies. They are required to help people locate the information they need for their work. They could also be responsible for online data services such as intranets (internal corporate internets).

Entry qualifications

To become a 'chartered librarian', the recognised professional qualification, you must qualify for membership of the Chartered Institute of Library and Information Professionals (CILIP). This was formed in 2002 from a merger of the Library Association and the Institute of Information Scientists. Unless you have a CILIP accredited first degree (available at 14 UK colleges and universities), you will need to supplement the degree you do have with a one-year, full-time or two-year, part-time postgraduate course. You then undertake a minimum of one year's post-course training.

CILIP also runs a jobsite for those seeking vacancies, on www.lisjobnet.com

Further information

CILIP – 7 Ridgmount Street, London WC1E 7AE. Tel: 020 7255 0500. www.cilip.org.uk

In Scotland:

CILIP – 1st Floor Building C, Brandon Gate, Leechlee Road, Hamilton ML3 6AU. Tel: 01698 458888. www.slainte.org.uk

In Wales:

CILIP – c/o Department of Information and Library Studies, University of Wales Aberystwyth, Llanbadarn Fawr, Aberystwyth, Ceredigon SY23 3AS. Tel: 01970 622174. www.dis.aber.ac.uk/cilip_w/index.htm

In Ireland:

> **CILIP** – BELB, 40 Academy Street, Belfast, Northern Ireland
> BT1 2NQ. Tel: 028 9056 4011. www.cilip.org.uk/ireland

Researchers

Researchers are used by a wide variety of organisations from government departments to trade unions, from political parties to market research companies.

In government you would normally be working within a government department and handling external and internal research enquiries, which could come from colleagues, other government departments, academics, local councils, regional development agencies and members of the public. A lot of the work would be desk research in libraries, but you would use a variety of other techniques including surveys. You could also find yourself briefing, orally or in writing, senior colleagues and government ministers on the research evidence that you have found. On occasions you might also have to present papers at conferences.

You might also become a social researcher for other kinds of government agency, trades unions, and commercial firms, including market research agencies. Although any degree is normally acceptable, employers do prefer social scientists. The content of the work is not dissimilar to that noted above and after getting a brief from your client you might use a variety of research techniques to get the relevant information. These could include desk research, quantitative and qualitative research, questionnaires and so on. With some agencies this could include developing and testing new theories.

There is also political research. Many members of parliament and senior party officials start this way. Apart from examining political issues in depth, you would monitor the media and *Hansard* (which reports parliamentary debates verbatim) to spot emerging political issues and to identify possible lines of attack that could be used against your party's rivals. You will also prepare briefs and policy papers as well as ghost articles and speeches for your party's MPs.

Although political researchers are usually associated with the House of Commons – the House of Lords, the European Parliament and the Scottish Parliament also use researchers.

Political researchers have less job security than others, because the various political parties recruit significant numbers of researchers in the build-up to a general election, but then shed many of them when the election is over. However, for those with political ambitions, it is perhaps the most reliable entry into Westminster.

Further information

The Market Research Society – 15 Northburgh Street, London EC1V 0JR. Tel: 020 7490 4911. www.mrs.org.uk

The National Centre for Social Research – 35 Northampton Square, London EC1V OAX. Tel: 020 7250 1866. www.natcen.ac.uk

Office for National Statistics – Customer Contact Centre, Room 1.015, Cardiff Road, Newport NP10 8XG. Tel: 0845 601 3034. www.statistics.gov.uk

The Social Research Association – PO Box 33660, London N16 6WE. Tel: 020 8880 5684. www.the-sra.org.uk

Chapter nine
Careers using archaeology

What image do you have of archaeologists? Do you see Indiana Jones pursuing ancient treasures in competition with hordes of villains? Or do you see a team fronted by Tony Robinson on a two-day dig for television's *Time Team* series? Or perhaps, more mundanely, do you see someone supervising a crowd of volunteers excavating ruins with trowels and soft paint brushes, or picture a lone expert poring over bits of broken pottery and other artefacts in the back room of a museum?

Archaeology does have its moments of high drama. In 1922, Howard Carter was excavating in the Valley of the Kings in Egypt. A staircase of 16 steps was uncovered in the sand leading down to a sloping rubble-filled rock tunnel 30 feet long. They cleared the tunnel, at the end of which was a blocked doorway. With three companions beside him, Carter prised out some of the stones and inserted a candle through the hole. What he saw is best described in his own words.

'At first I could see nothing, the hot air from the chamber causing the candle to flicker, but presently, as my eyes grew accustomed to the light, details of the room within emerged slowly from the mist, strange animals, statues and gold – everywhere the glint of gold. For the moment – an eternity it must have seemed to the others standing by – I was struck dumb with amazement, and when Lord Carnarvon, unable to stand the suspense any longer, enquired anxiously, 'Can you see anything?' it was all I could do to get out the words, 'Yes, wonderful things'.'

Howard Carter, Egyptologist

He had found the tomb of Tutankhamun – four chambers, hewn from rock, containing treasure of unimagined magnificence.

Although such spectacular finds are rare they are not unique. Just think about the buried terra cotta army at Qin in China, or the vivid Palaeolithic paintings in the Lascaux cave in France. Archaeology is all about discovery.

Archaeology is the study of our human past through physical remains. These range from buried cities to microscopic organisms. Archaeology is the only source of information about much of our history – especially about those times before written records were kept. Everything we know about the beginning of agriculture, the origin of towns and the discovery of metals comes from physical remains. It was the discovery, in the 1850s, of flint tools beneath the bones of extinct animals that first showed man had lived many thousands of years before the beginning of history as it was then known. It was this sort of evidence that eventually led to the general acceptance of Charles Darwin's theory of evolution.

Archaeology is growing in popularity, largely thanks to television documentaries. This has two consequences. To be accepted for a degree course you'll need three A levels or three to four Scottish Highers or equivalent, often at a high grade. And when you do qualify, you'll find there are more archaeology graduates than there are relevant jobs. Most people graduating in archaeology have to follow another career.

This shouldn't discourage you from studying archaeology if the subject interests you. It combines practical and theoretical skills, gives you practice in the collection and analysis of data, and provides you with experience of team working when carrying out field projects. All of these skills are attractive to employers in other areas, especially industry and commerce. However, in this chapter we will concentrate on working as an archaeologist.

Working as an archaeologist

Archaeology involves far more than digging up artefacts on historic sites. The work of the archaeologist may start with trying to locate a site. Some sites are discovered by accident – perhaps in the course of development work, such as building a road. On other occasions, archaeologists may suspect the existence of buried remains of historic importance.

Locating such a site precisely may entail careful research, such as the study of aerial photographs and the use of remote sensing methods. Plotting and analysing increasingly involves computer-based techniques. Geophysical procedures, adapted from oil and mineral prospecting, can also reveal much of the layout of the hidden remains before digging begins.

Once digging starts, the position of every object found has to be precisely plotted in three dimensions. The position of an object, both on the site and in relation to other finds, often reveals more than the object itself. This is why archaeologists get so upset with amateurs using metal detectors to locate and dig up finds.

All sites are built up from an accumulation of sediments. These may be the result of either the decay of buildings and other man-made remains or the development of soils and vegetation over the site. The study of these sediments can yield vital clues to the history of the site. For example, the study of pollen grains can reveal changes in the vegetation. This in turn gives evidence for changes in the climate of the site.

Many delicate artefacts are preserved in the soil or under water, and start to decay as soon as they are exposed to the air. Conservation – preserving and caring for objects so that they survive after excavation – is a vital part of archaeological work. Finds have to be catalogued, photographed, drawn (drawings often reveal details not seen in photographs) and examined. Artefacts are studied, physically and chemically, to find out how they were made and to identify the origin of the raw materials. They also have to be dated, using a range of radiocarbon and other techniques. As you can see, archaeology spans the arts and sciences. Conservation and the examination of artefacts are usually carried out in laboratories by those who have studied science-based archaeology.

All aspects of the project must be written up (and ideally published) in order to give other scholars access to the work.

Archaeologists tend to specialise in their work (over 80 specialisms have been identified). Archaeologists can specialise geographically, chronologically (such as prehistory, Roman, Anglo-Saxon etc) or technically (such as site surveying, excavation, studying artefacts and so on).

Working for an archaeological body

There are six main public archaeological bodies in the UK: English Heritage (merged in 1999 with The Royal Commission on the Historical Monuments of England); Historic Scotland; The Royal Commission on the Ancient and Historical Monuments of Scotland; Cadw (Welsh Historic Monuments); The Royal Commission on the Ancient and Historical Monuments of Wales; and The Environment and Heritage Service of Northern Ireland. Each is responsible for the long-term conservation of ancient monuments and historic buildings, for promoting the public's understanding and enjoyment of our historic heritage, and for compiling and making available records of all the ancient monuments and sites in each country.

They employ Inspectors of Ancient Monuments who deal with the preservation and protection of sites and monuments, monitor fieldwork projects and recommend grant aid. Historic Buildings Inspectors, who have specialist knowledge of architecture or art history, do similar work for buildings. Much of the work involves advising people and writing reports. Inspectors usually cover large geographical areas, so they tend to do a lot of travelling.

English Heritage has sections concerned with the conservation of finds, illustration and publication. It also runs a Central Archaeology Service to advise on the archaeological activities it funds and to provide a mobile team for surveys and excavations.

Other employers

The National Trust, The National Trust for Scotland, the national parks, local authorities and utility companies (like the water supply companies) employ archaeologists to record, survey and, occasionally, excavate sites in their care.

All counties in England and Wales, and most in Scotland, employ a Sites and Monuments Officer, usually with a small staff, who acts as a curator for the area's archaeology and maintains a database called the Sites and Monuments Record (SMR) or the Heritage Environment Record (HER). They also advise on the recording and conservation of historic remains when planning applications are being considered, and ensure that fieldwork by independent bodies is carried out to a satisfactory standard. Most fieldwork that becomes necessary through development is undertaken by teams attached to independent bodies. These range from museums or local authorities to universities, independent trusts or charities.

Museums also offer a range of posts. Although there may be some fieldwork, keepers are more often responsible for the care or storage of artefacts, for research and for handling enquiries from the public, including identifying objects that people bring in. Archaeologists may also work on interpretive displays to explain finds to the public. You might also find that curatorship is a suitable career – see Chapter ten for further information.

Entry qualifications

Although archaeology is an arts and humanities subject, it links with many disciplines including physics, chemistry, biology, geology, technology, the medical sciences, mathematics and geography as well as history, art, social science and religion. You can take either a BA or a BSc degree in archaeology, the BSc concentrating on archaeological science. However, you must realise that most BA degrees will involve some archaeological science, even though a science subject at A level or at Scottish Higher level isn't usually a requirement for entry to a course.

To work as a professional archaeologist, you'll normally need a degree in archaeology although other disciplines are sometimes accepted. It is immensely valuable to have experience of fieldwork (most degree courses include some field projects). Indeed, it's a good idea to join an archaeology society or the Young Archaeologists Club before you start your degree, and to take part in digs or other fieldwork, or to do voluntary work in a museum. University admissions tutors will want evidence of your interest in the subject, so this could also help you to win a place on a degree course.

IT skills are valuable, as computers are used increasingly to store and analyse data. Some archaeologists also use computer-aided design (CAD) in reconstruction work, producing three-dimensional images of sites or objects from incomplete data.

The Institute of Field Archaeologists (IFA) is the recognised professional institute, and many employers of archaeologists give preference to its members. Membership is based on academic qualifications, experience and documented achievements.

To work on excavations, you need to be in robust health. Working on digs in all weathers can be tough. Because you're trying to build up a picture of the past from many thousands of tiny bits of evidence, you must be painstakingly methodical and thorough. Patience and determination are essential. Howard Carter had five years of fruitless digging in the Valley of the Kings before the steps to Tutankhamun's tomb emerged from the sand.

You should be a good team worker and have leadership potential. You'll have to collaborate with other disciplines, especially scientists, and you may have to supervise teams working on site. You'll also need to communicate clearly and lucidly – orally and in writing. Some archaeologists specialise in underwater sites. They may work on sunken ships, like the Mary Rose, or on sites that have become flooded or sunk beneath the sea. To work on these excavations you would, of course, need additional skills.

Career development

The Council for British Archaeology warns that 'outside the national agencies (like English Heritage), local authorities and universities, jobs tend to be short term and career prospects limited'. Archaeology is a very small profession. A survey in 2002 estimated that there were 776 organisations employing 5,700 archaeologists. However, the Council says that those who are committed and persevere often manage to make a career in archaeology.

If you aim to be an excavation archaeologist, you will need to work your way up through the ranks – from excavator to site assistant to supervisor and so on. The main qualification for advancement is practical experience.

In English Heritage and the Royal Commissions, you start as an assistant. Although much of the work is administrative, site experience is valuable if you are to progress to senior posts. Museums have their own career structure.

Finding vacancies

More than 140 organisations – including most councils, major units and national archaeological bodies advertise their vacancies through the British Archaeological Jobs Resource (BAJR) website, at www.bajr.org

The Institute of Field Archaeologists also runs a subscription Job Information Service (JIS). This produces a weekly bulletin and an online service that reproduces advertisements placed by employers and all archaeological, heritage and research opportunities appearing in the national press and specialist journals during that week. See the website, at www.archaeologists.net

You're also likely to find suitable jobs advertised in *The Guardian, The Independent,* and in *The Museums Journal.*

Archaeology Abroad publishes two bulletins annually (April and November) that advertises around 1000 places a year for volunteers, professional staff and specialists on a wide variety of projects of all periods. See the website, at www.britarch.ac.uk/archabroad

Further information

Association of National Park Authorities – 126 Bute Street, Cardiff CF10 5LE. Tel: 029 2049 9966. www.anpa.gov.uk

British Archaeological Job Resource – 5/2 Hamilton Terrace, Edinburgh EH15 1NB. Tel: 0131 669 2683. wwwbajr.co.uk

Council for British Archaeology – St. Mary's House, 66 Bootham, York YO30 7BZ. Tel: 01904 671417. www.britarch.ac.uk

Cultural Heritage National Training Organisation – 7 Burnett Street, Little Germany, Bradford BD1 5BJ. Tel: 01274 391056. www.chnto.co.uk

English Heritage – Customer Services Department, PO Box 569, Swindon SN2 2YP. Tel: 0870 333 1181. www.english-heritage.org.uk

Forestry Commission – Silvan House, 231 Corstorphine Rd, Edinburgh EH12 7AT. Tel: 0131 334 0303. www.forestry.gov.uk

Institute of Field Archaeologists – SHES, Whiteknights, University of Reading, PO Box 227, Reading RG6 6AB. Tel: 0118 378 6446. www.archaelogists.net

The National Trust – 36 Queen Anne's Gate, London SW1H 9AS. Tel: 020 7447 6620. www.nationaltrust.org.uk

National Trust for Scotland – Wemyss House, 28 Charlotte Square, Edinburgh EH2 4ET. Tel: 0131 243 9300. www.nts.org.uk

Chapter ten
Careers using history

'Ignorance of history is to remain always a child.'

Cicero, Roman statesman

Many students have repeated Henry Ford's phrase – 'history is bunk'. But most employers would disagree, because history is widely accepted as a rigorous intellectual discipline. So it is welcomed for entry into most areas of industry, commerce and public service.

The main vocational value of studying history is that it provides good training in gathering, sorting and analysing information and ideas, often from incomplete sources, and explaining things in clear English. In most fields, historians are valued for their intellectual discipline and skills, not for their specialist knowledge. However, employers are seldom impressed by a degree made up of several modules covering different periods and topics. You would be wise to specialise in one or, at most, two themes. It is the ability to sustain an in-depth study that will impress most employers.

As well as teaching, there are some other careers in which you can use your specialist knowledge of historical subjects. The main ones are working in museums, art galleries and archives. There may also be a few openings in archaeology, particularly if you've a relevant postgraduate qualification – see Chapter nine.

Museum and art gallery work

The work of museums and art galleries is very similar and often overlaps. Museums collect, document, preserve, exhibit, interpret and store materials of historical, scientific and cultural interest. Art galleries do the same for paintings, sculpture and other works of art. Some institutions, like the Victoria and Albert Museum in London, are both a museum and an art gallery.

There are nearly 3,000 museums and art galleries in Britain, collectively employing around 13,000 curators and managers. Museums are no longer the dusty repositories of artefacts. They increasingly are part of the leisure industry and aim to entertain as well as inform visitors. Displays are now far more imaginative than in the past. And art galleries too have improved their displays with better lighting, improved labelling and with exhibitions on particular themes and on individual artists.

Because many aspects of the work are very similar, for the purpose of this chapter both types of institution are referred to as museums.

There are four main types of museum, and although you may move from one to another during your career, you will find that attitudes and working conditions vary. The four types are:

- national
- university
- local authority
- independent.

National museums

The Government largely funds these, although most have to raise extra money through book and souvenir sales, sponsorship and so on. The national museums include the British Museum, the National Gallery, the Natural History Museum, the Tate Galleries and the National Museums of Scotland and Wales as well as 'outstations' (sites away from the main body of the museum) such as the Science Museum's National Railway Museum at York. These national museums provide about half of all museum jobs. Although they are officially independent of government, the terms of employment are similar to those in the Civil Service.

University museums

Most university museums are departmental collections used for teaching. These are staffed by university lecturers or laboratory technicians, who combine museum work with their other duties. However, there is a handful of large university museums that are open to the public and which employ full-time curators, such as the Ashmolean in Oxford, the Fitzwilliam in Cambridge and the Hunterian in Glasgow.

Local authority museums

There are some 700 local authority museums. These range from famous museums like the Museum of London, Manchester City Art Gallery and the Burrell Collection in Glasgow, through to small museums of local history with only one or two staff. In these, you're employed on the same conditions as other local authority staff.

Independent museums

The largest growing group is the independent museums. These are funded by admission charges, grants, endowments and sponsorship. They have to be commercially successful, and so are run much more as businesses than other museums. They include sophisticated tourist attractions like the Jorvik Viking Centre in York and the Ironbridge Gorge Museum, as well as hundreds of small special interest ones.

Terms and conditions of employment vary. In general, commercial and communication skills are as important as academic qualifications.

There are a variety of jobs available in museums, particularly in the larger institutions. These range from uniformed attendants to museum designers and shop sales staff. As a graduate in history or art history you're most likely to be interested in an educational role or in curatorship.

Education officers

Many museums employ education staff. Education officers teach classes in the museum and in schools or colleges. They also prepare teaching materials for school projects, hold workshops for teachers on how to make the best of the museum, run holiday events for young people and organise guided tours and talks.

Curatorship

The main concern of curators is to look after the museum's collections. You'd be responsible for acquiring objects and for researching, cataloguing, storing, displaying and explaining them. In the largest museums these would be your only duties and you might be able to specialise. But in most you'd be involved in all sorts of other jobs too, fund raising, answering visitor queries, security, setting up and publicising special exhibitions, giving talks and writing about the collection. In the smallest museums you might have to do all these things. Note that only the big national museums and the largest local authority museums offer positions where research is a major part of the job. As a curator in most museums you are not only responsible for the care of the collections, but must manage the museum or your department within it. This can include administration and managing staff.

Entry qualifications

To become an education officer, a teaching or community education background is usually required and your chances will be improved if you have successful teaching experience and an understanding of the

National Curriculum. You can find more on teaching in Chapter five. It is increasingly important for education officer and curator posts that you have prior work experience in the field as a volunteer. This will not only give you invaluable experience and a network of contacts, but will normally be expected by museum and art gallery recruiters.

To become a curator or art gallery keeper in a national or local authority museum you'll normally need, in addition to a degree, a postgraduate qualification in museum studies or a related subject. Although a higher degree isn't mandatory, nine in ten curators and keepers have one.

Independent museums don't always ask for academic qualifications, but it is very helpful to have them as the competition for jobs is so fierce. These museums will also tend to look for commercial and communication skills. Local authority and independent museums use a lot of voluntary workers, and again you will almost certainly be expected to have experience as a volunteer worker before you are accepted into a full-time paid post.

The personal qualities required for curators differ somewhat between the types of museum. But there are some common aspects. You need intellectual curiosity and must enjoy knowledge for its own sake. You must be a good organiser. You should be able to communicate your specialist knowledge clearly, lucidly and enthusiastically to non-specialists. And you must have an empathy with your visitors and know what they want.

Training and career development

If you are interested in museum work you should join the Museums Association. This confers many benefits, including free or discounted admission to most museums, training courses and much more.

The largest museums have well-established career structures and you can progress internally. Your career may lead from assistant curator/ keeper through ranks of increasing seniority up to director with responsibility for running the whole museum. However, administration and management jobs are increasingly seen as distinct from that of curator. The directors of some national museums have been appointed from outside the museum world. However, most senior post-holders, including the directors of most museums, begin their career as curators. Elsewhere you are most likely to progress your career by moving from one museum to another, taking care of larger collections or possibly developing as a specialist. Because staff turnover tends to be low, progression is often slow.

Finding vacancies

Members of the Museums Association can firstly check for vacancies on the Association's website, at www.museumsassociation.org Most posts for curators are advertised in *Museums Journal* (published by the Museums Association), but also look in the national press, usually *The Guardian* (Mondays) and *The Times Higher Education Supplement*. Check regional papers for jobs in local authority museums.

It may be worth looking at the opportunities with English Heritage (and its equivalents in Scotland, Wales and Northern Ireland), The National Trust and The National Trust for Scotland. These bodies preserve nationally important monuments and historic buildings (and sometimes their contents). Although not museums, some of these organisations have openings for history graduates, for example, as education officers or site custodians. Chapter nine offers more information about fieldwork opportunities with these bodies.

Archivists

Archivists preserve historical records. Although most people think in terms of ancient documents, contemporary material is also preserved for future use. Because there is a substantial overlap between the work of archivists and that of librarians and information professionals, you should also refer back to Chapter eight.

Apart from documents, modern records can include microfilm, audio and video recordings, CDs, and so on. Material can be found in a variety of sources, including the records of:

■ central and local government

■ courts of law

- universities

- professional institutions (such as The Law Society)

- business firms.

Archives may also include private papers such as title deeds, family papers and the diaries and letters of notable people. As an archivist you'll be involved in the study and selection of material, deciding what is worth preserving for posterity. It is impractical to keep every document produced. You will take responsibility for the preservation, arrangement and description of the material for future reference purposes. You'll be required to assist people using the archives, whether they are academics researching a particular subject, members of the public tracing their family history, students working on a thesis, or lawyers looking for evidence to support a client's case.

Most archivists work for central or local government. There are major archives of state and other papers held at the Public Records Office, split between sites in Kew and central London. Local archives are situated around the country. There are also limited openings in other organisations, including professional institutions, universities, libraries, specialist museums, industry and research bodies. Some of the work at these places will extend into information management. You'll find more detail on library and information work in Chapter eight.

Entry qualifications and training

You must have a good honours degree in history and you will normally need an MA or postgraduate Diploma in Archives and Records Management. Relevant work experience – paid or unpaid – is often required before you start postgraduate studies. Some institutions offer one-year paid graduate traineeships (see the Society of Archivists website, listed below).

Apart from a strong sense of history, you'll need to be curious and to enjoy painstaking research. A meticulous eye for detail is vital. Because you will be responsible for the physical care of the records (and some old documents are very fragile) you'll need an aptitude for practical tasks. To help people conduct their research you must also be a skilled communicator; you must also be patient as they won't always know precisely what they're looking for!

A part-time training course, 'Certificate in Archive Conservation', is run by the Society of Archivists but is available only to working archivists.

Finding vacancies

This is a very small profession and the supply and demand for archivists just about balance. Vacancies are scarce in some parts of the country. You'll usually need to go wherever there is a vacancy – both for your first job and to develop your career. Only a handful of universities run postgraduate courses for archivists. Consequently, most employers with vacancies will target those institutions. You're most likely to find your first post either through your academic department, which will be in contact with most potential employers, or through your university careers service.

Vacancies are advertised on the Society of Archivists website (see below) but some are also in *The Times* and in *The Guardian*.

'...it is only through knowledge of its history that a society can have knowledge of itself. As a man without memory and self-knowledge is a man adrift, so a society without memory (or more correctly, without recollection) and self-knowledge would be a society adrift.'

Arthur Marwick, in The Nature of History

Jennie Hood

Jennie, 26, is using her interest in history through working as an archive assistant.

Career profile

Job title: archive assistant

Employer: Cheshire Record Office

A levels: English literature, history, art, general studies and archaeology

Degree: BA history

University: Manchester

Postgraduate qualification: MA Victorian studies, University College Chester

'I've had a love of history since I was a child, and used to help out at the local museum in my summer holidays. And I thought for a degree it was very important to do something that I was interested in and something that I'd enjoy.

I had no idea of what I wanted to do on graduation. The point of doing history was that I think it is very important to know about the past to understand why society is like it is today.

I took a higher degree for a variety of reasons. Firstly, I enjoy studying and love learning. I became really interested in the Victorian period in my third year, and wanted to learn more. I looked at various MA courses, but the only Victorian studies course I could find was here in Chester. It was a super course. I also thought that an MA would help me to get a better job right away – although it didn't!

I didn't have a job while doing my first degree, but when I did my MA I worked full time in a Starbucks café just to pay for it. I got to be a supervisor – managing people, controlling cash and had control of the safe and so on. That experience helped me to get other jobs.

When I'd finished my MA I'd had five years of continuous studying and thought I needed a break. I went off travelling to Australia and New Zealand for a few months. When I got back I did a CELTA course (Certificate in English Language

Teaching for Adults). If I go travelling again it's something I can use. If you go to language school anywhere in the world that is the qualification they ask for. That took me two months part time while I worked in a pub.

When I started my proper job search my ideal job would have been working in a gallery or museum. But I never realised that you need specialist qualifications. I didn't have particularly good careers advice at school or university. So I just started applying for all sorts of things. You get to a point where you think: I've got to do something just to earn money.

Last year I saw an advertisement for an archivist at Hawarden in Flintshire. I didn't get that, but they offered me a temporary contract on a special project that Flintshire had going. They were organising their records for the Freedom of Information Act. This involved cataloguing all of their records – from the 19th century to really modern records. What they had done over the years was to put things in boxes, stack them and put them away. Everybody had forgotten what they contained. So it was our job to look at them, enter them on spreadsheets and assess their historical importance. I think it was good for them to have somebody with a history degree to assess how important the documents are going to be in the future.

The job was planned to last four months, but they hugely underestimated the volume of records and it ended up as ten months. Then I saw a job for an archive assistant in Chester. I applied, had the interview and started a few days later.

I work in the search room. When I'm on the enquiry desk I help people who are doing their family histories, research for their degrees, and all sorts of things. So I'm there to help them with their enquiries and show them where everything is. If I'm on document production I get the documents out of the strong room for them, sort out any copying and get orders sent off. So it's a very varied job. I absolutely love it. I've finally found something that I want to do for a career.

I've started right at the bottom, but you can work your way up by doing a proper archive qualification and become an archivist. It's very competitive, 65 people applied for the job I've got.

What advice would I give someone thinking of reading history? If you enjoy it, do it – because you'll regret it if you don't. However, you can do qualifications until you're blue in the face, but it's experience that counts. It can be very difficult to get into anything if you don't have experience of doing relevant voluntary work.'

Further information

Associations of Independent Museums – London Transport Museum, Covent Garden, London WC2E 7BB. Tel: 020 7379 6344. www.aimus.org.uk

Cultural Heritage National Training Organisation – First Floor, Glyde House, Glydegate, Bradford BD5 0UP. Tel: 01274 391056. www.chnto.co.uk

The Museums Association – 42 Clerkenwell Close, London EC1R 0PA. Tel: 020 7430 0730. www.museumassociation.org

Society of Archivists – Prioryfield House, 20 Cannon Street, Taunton, Somerset TA1 1SW. Tel: 01823 327030. www.archives.org.uk

Chapter eleven
Careers using languages and linguistics

You may choose to study a foreign language because you are interested in the literature and culture of another country, or perhaps because it can give you opportunities for travel, or because it opens up your career options. With the eastward expansion of the European Union and the growing globalisation of business, a language would appear to open up many fresh job opportunities. Yet recent research shows that the total numbers of students studying degree courses in foreign languages has declined 14% in the past five years. And the numbers sitting foreign language GCSEs has similarly fallen over the same period. This is astonishing in a country that has traded globally for centuries and which depends on exports for its economic survival.

As a Nuffield Foundation inquiry recently showed, Britain is 'monolingual and dangerously complacent about it'. Although English is now the most widely used international business language, only one in eight of the world's population speaks any English at all. Moreover, most English speakers are in the UK, North America, Africa, Australasia and the Indian subcontinent. But the world's richest economies outside North America, as well as those with the greatest prospects of growth, are almost all non-English speaking.

In a global economy, businesses that don't grasp export opportunities are at a big disadvantage. A quarter of British firms report that their main obstacle to exporting is their lack of language skills. Other studies show that only just over a third of UK firms employing up to 500 people have an executive able to negotiate in another language. In contrast, 90% of executives in similar sized companies in many European countries can do so. Two-thirds of these European companies have at least one executive who can negotiate in more than one foreign language. In most European business circles you're considered illiterate if you don't speak at least one foreign language fluently.

'I speak Spanish to God, Italian to women, French to men, and German to my horse.'

Charles V, Holy Roman Emperor

To compete effectively in international markets, we need people who can do business in the major non-English speaking markets – particularly with the rest of the European Union (including the new members in Eastern Europe), but also in the Far East (especially China) and South America. Managers from these countries may sell to us in excellent English, but when we want them as customers they expect us to sell to them in their own language.

In spite of all this, UK employers still give very low priority to language skills. For example, the Association of Graduate Recruiters recently asked its members to rate the importance of 19 different graduate skills. Foreign language skills rated a depressing 19th, and cultural sensitivity not much better in 16th place.

Because at present a language skill is seldom seen as useful, it's not usually enough to take a modern languages degree on its own to enter graduate-level work. There are four exceptions to this:

- teaching languages (see Chapter five)
- teaching English as a foreign language (TEFL)
- interpreting
- translating.

If you want to work with a language outside these areas you really need to complement it with other vocational skills. Fortunately, you can study most modern languages with an amazing range of options.

There are many other occupations in which a language is an asset or even a requirement, but it is not the main skill, and may not even be part of your day-to-day work. They include, for instance, broadcasting, the European civil service, the diplomatic service, export marketing, librarianship, law, journalism, banking, insurance, accountancy, and travel and tourism. Your language skills can enhance your prospects in any of these careers, but your language ability will be secondary to the other skills of the job.

If you are studying linguistics, either on its own or as part of your modern languages degree, you may also be able to train as a speech and language therapist. This is covered at the end of the chapter.

Teaching English as a foreign language

This involves teaching people from other countries to speak and write in English – although the emphasis is often on speech. It helps to be fluent in the language of your students, hence your own need for a language. Your students are likely to be adults and may be taught abroad or in the UK. They may be recent immigrants, students wanting to study at a British or North American university, or business people who need to learn English.

Most openings for teaching English as a foreign language (TEFL) are abroad, mainly in Western Europe and the Middle East. Women should be aware that some Middle Eastern countries accept only men. There are also opportunities in UK colleges of further education and particularly in commercial language schools. UK posts are more difficult to find and may require a Postgraduate Certificate in Education (PGCE), previous experience, or both. Students may wish to learn English for career reasons, to study at a British institution, or for leisure purposes. You might also work as a TESL (teaching English as a second language) teacher. This work tends to be with newly arrived immigrants (including refugees) or ethnic minorities in the UK.

As part of a languages degree you might spend a period working abroad as an 'assistant', teaching English to secondary school students. This gives you a flavour of teaching work, and also allows you to learn something of the culture of the host country.

Entry qualifications and career development

You don't need a teaching qualification, or even – for some commercial colleges – a degree, to teach English as a foreign language. But if you ever want to return to mainstream teaching in Britain, it is wise to take the Postgraduate Certificate in Education (PGCE). PGCE and diploma courses with an emphasis on teaching English as a foreign language or as a second language are available at several universities and colleges. The most widely recognised entry qualification for both TEFL and TESL in the UK is the Cambridge Certificate in English Language Teaching for Adults (CELTA). Courses in teaching are also offered in some private language schools, but these can be costly.

Outside mainstream teaching, there are few opportunities for career progression. This is why it's advisable to get the PGCE.

Finding vacancies

Posts are advertised in *EFL Gazette* and *Overseas Jobs Express*, on the internet (try www.britishcouncil.org.uk and also the Association of Registered English Language Services (ARELS) on www.arels.org.uk) and in the national press, particularly *The Guardian* (Tuesday) and *The Times Higher Educational Supplement*. One of the largest employers is The British Council – which promotes Britain abroad in 110 countries. In Britain, the main employers are colleges of further education and private language schools.

The terms and conditions of work vary a lot. In colleges of further education, you work normal college hours and, in addition, may have to do evening work. In private colleges the hours tend to be longer and the holidays shorter. Some employ you on a 'self-employed' basis – which means you are paid by the lesson. Overseas contracts are often for a fixed term, but may include accommodation and paid visits home.

Interpreting

There are two forms of interpretation – consecutive and simultaneous. In the first you listen to a speech, either in part or whole, and then relay it to the audience. This may mean taking notes as reminders of what was said. This method is slow, because the audience must listen to the original then the translation (or even translations!).

Simultaneous interpretation involves translating what you hear immediately to your audience as the speaker continues to talk. You may do this on a one-to-one basis, known as 'whispering' because you whisper your interpretation into your client's ear. More often simultaneous work involves sitting in a soundproof booth and listening to the speaker through headphones. You speak your interpretation into a microphone that feeds your voice to the headphones of your audience.

Simultaneous interpretation is generally accepted as the more stressful work, because there is almost no thinking time. To ease the pressure, two interpreters often work together, alternating in sessions lasting perhaps half-an-hour. But, this isn't always the case. Interpreters can sometimes work three hours or more without a break.

In either form of interpretation, you must have an excellent knowledge of both languages. There are many words and sayings in any language, which can't be translated directly into another, so you must be able to give far more than just a literal translation. The only full-time work for interpreters is in 'conference interpreting', and this is a tiny profession. Conference interpreters always work from the foreign or 'passive' language into their own or 'active' language.

Most conference interpreters work for international bodies such as the United Nations and its many agencies, the institutions of the European Union, NATO, and so on. As an interpreter you may have to travel worldwide to translate at the conferences and meetings attended by representatives of such bodies. There are also self-employed interpreters and those employed by specialist communications agencies. Both tend to do other interpreting and translation work in addition to conference work. They too are expected to travel in pursuit of their work. This may be attractive at first, but the novelty eventually wears off. The life is physically and mentally demanding.

Businesses also need interpreters, for example during trade fairs, when receiving delegations from abroad and in negotiating overseas contracts. In this case you will translate both ways – into and out of your own language. This is usually part-time self-employed work, although some companies are large enough to require full-time interpreters.

If you can speak a language used by UK immigrants and refugees – such as Pashto (from Afghanistan), Hindi (India), Urdu (Pakistan) and Albanian – you may find work (usually self-employed or part-time) helping local authority departments, the courts, medical staff and the police.

Translating

To be a good translator, it is not enough to have a good knowledge of languages. You must be able to translate idiomatically and to write lucidly and succinctly. Translators work into their own language. The work is usually of two types – literary or technical and commercial.

Literary translation

This covers novels, poetry, plays, biographies and similar material. Almost all translators in this field are self-employed and few can make a living this way. The work is generally very difficult, because you must catch the 'spirit' not just the literal meaning of the work. You are producing a paraphrase rather than a translation.

'Some hold translations not unlike to be
The wrong side of a Turkish tapestry'

**James Howell, 17th-century writer, royal historian and
translator**

To take an example, here are two versions of the opening verse of the Rubáiyát of Omar Khayyám, both translated from the original Persian by Edward Fitzgerald:

'Awake! For Morning in the Bowl of Night
Has flung the Stone that puts the Stars to Flight:
And Lo! the Hunter of the East has caught
The Sultan's Turret in a Noose of Light.'

'Wake! For the Sun behind yon Eastern height
Has chased the Session of the Stars from Night;
And, to the field of Heav'n ascending strikes
The Sultan's Turret with a Shaft of Light.'

You can see from these passages an example of what variations may be offered for a single text.

Technical and commercial translation

This is more straightforward and offers the best work prospects. However, you'll need a detailed knowledge of a specialised field such as law, medicine, science or engineering, or of business usage. Accuracy is the most important aspect of this work. Work can range from translations of books, through scientific papers and legal contracts, to technical manuals. Most of the work is done on a freelance basis, although some translators are full-time employees. Most of the latter work for international bodies such as the United Nations and European Union and for larger government departments and the Government Communications Headquarters (GCHQ).

Entry qualifications

For translators and interpreters each organisation has its own requirements. Those employing interpreters usually want two languages other than English, but not necessarily at degree level. A languages degree could be followed by a postgraduate qualification in interpreting. International organisations like the EU and UN usually conduct their own entry tests.

Training and career development

There is no standard training, although a postgraduate qualification can be helpful. There are specialist courses in interpreting and translation. These include: a one-year MA in interpreting and translation at Bradford University; an MA in conference interpretation at Westminster University, the only UK course recognised by AIIC (Association Internationale des Interprètes de Conférence) (see under finding vacancies below); and an MA and Postgraduate Diploma in translating and interpreting at Salford University.

Most interpreters and translators start in other careers where they can use their languages and do freelance interpreting and translation on the side. As their skills improve, they may continue to work as a freelance or they may try to enter one of the organisations recruiting full-time staff. Such opportunities are few and far between. Although there is no formal career development, earnings for the successful can be relatively high. However, for most people in translation and interpreting work, the life is an uncertain one.

Finding vacancies

Most permanent posts are advertised in the national press or on the internet. Your best chance for freelance work is to register with an agency. If you want to work in conference interpreting, you should become a member of AIIC. AIIC is the professional body for the industry. It holds examinations, determines qualifications and sets standards in terms of both pay and conditions and guaranteed quality of work. Most organisations prefer to use AIIC interpreters because they will be assured of their professional capability. AIIC is an international organisation with members in over 65 countries.

Further information

Association Internationale des Interprètes de Conférence – 10 Avenue de Sécheron, CH-1202, Geneva, Switzerland. Tel: 0041 22 908 1540. www.aiic.net

Chartered Institute of Linguists – Saxon House, 48 Southwark Street, London SE1 1UN. Tel: 020 7940 3100. www.iol.org.uk

Institute of Translation and Interpreting – Fortuna House, South Fifth Street, Milton Keynes MK9 2EU. Tel: 01908 325250. www.iti.org.uk

International Association of Teachers of EFL – Darwin College, University of Kent, Canterbury CT2 7NY. Tel: 01227 824430. www.iatefl.org

CiLT, the National Centre for Languages (and incorporating the former Languages National Training Organisation) – 20 Bedfordbury, London WC2N 4LB. Tel: 020 7379 5101. www.cilt.org.uk

Using linguistics in your career

Linguistics is the scientific study of language. It involves the study of sounds and how they are made, grammatical constructions, and how meaning is conveyed. You may study linguistics as a subject in its own right, or as a specialist paper forming part of a modern languages degree. There are few occupations where you can use the subject directly, although linguistic theories are applied in various careers including teaching, social work and computing. For example, the computing industry aims to produce programs that will translate from one language to another. This calls for people who can analyse the structure of languages and design appropriate software. However, the career which will probably make most direct use of your specialist knowledge is speech and language therapy.

Speech and language therapy

Speech therapists assess and treat speech, language and voice defects of all kinds. The National Health Service employs the vast majority. They work in clinics, hospitals, special schools and patients' homes. Those working in rural areas may have a lot of travelling to do.

People are referred to speech therapists by their teachers, doctors or hospital consultants for a range of problems. A lot of the patients are children. They may be very slow in learning to talk, find it difficult to articulate or have a stammer or hearing difficulties. Many have physical or mental disabilities or are emotionally disturbed. Working with adults may involve helping people who have lost the ability to speak through illness or accident. Someone whose brain has been damaged through an accident or stroke may have to relearn how to speak and use language. People who have had their larynx (voice box) removed need to develop an alternative method of sound production. Although some people are treated in groups, most get individual treatment. Therapists also attend case conferences and must work closely with doctors, social workers, psychologists, teachers and other professionals.

To become a speech therapist, you'll need to understand people of all ages and temperaments and be able to win their confidence. You must communicate clearly. You need almost infinite patience because treatment can often be long and difficult. You will also need to be well organised because your work is largely unsupervised and you have to arrange your own schedules.

Entry, training and career development

The profession is open only to graduates, and speech therapists are recruited into the NHS only when trained and state registered. You can take an approved first-degree course at one of 16 universities and colleges. If you have a degree in a related subject, such as linguistics, you must undertake one of the five possible two-year Masters-level courses that are accredited by The Royal College of Speech and Language Therapists (RCSLT). You will then be eligible for the Certificate of Practice awarded by the College.

In the NHS, there is a promotion ladder of eight grades. The more senior you become, the more administration you will encounter.

Finding vacancies

Vacancies are advertised in the twice-monthly supplement to the RCSLT's *Bulletin*. The *Bulletin* and its supplements can also be viewed online by registered members of the RCSLT at the website listed below.

Further information

The Royal College of Speech and Language Therapists – 2 White Hart Yard, London SE1 1NX. Tel: 020 7378 1200. www.rcslt.org

Chapter twelve
Careers using theology and religious studies

'Men will wrangle for religion; write for it; fight for it; die for it; anything but live for it.'

The Reverend Charles C Colton, British author and clergyman

You don't have to be a believer to study theology or religious studies. The subjects are fascinating even if you have no faith or are a doubter. And the intellectual rigour of these subjects is recognised by most employers. However, the only career in which you can directly apply your theological knowledge, other than teaching, is the ministry. Because UK theology courses are geared to the Judaeo-Christian tradition, this chapter focuses on the ministry of those faiths. If you are interested in the ministry of other religions, see the notes near the end of this chapter.

The vocation

The ministry is not a career like any other. To start with, you have to believe in the teachings of your particular faith. You must have a sense of vocation (a call from God) and must be prepared to commit yourself to the service of God and your community. You must also accept that in some ways ministers are set apart from other people.

What do ministers do?

The work falls into two areas that might be described as ritual and pastoral. Many of the duties are common to all Christian denominations and Jewish traditions.

Ritual work

Ritual work covers religious rites and observance, including holding regular services, conducting marriages and funerals, and preaching. Far from being an empty formality, this aspect of the work is central to the ministry. It involves communicating the beliefs of your faith to people in ways they can understand, and encouraging them to recognise and use the gifts God has given them.

Pastoral work

Pastoral work involves caring for people in their daily lives. Typical activities include visiting the sick and the elderly, helping the homeless, comforting the bereaved, working with youth clubs and centres for the elderly, and aiding people with a variety of religious and personal problems. Rabbis are also involved in the social and often political life of their communities. Pastoral work is not limited to helping practising members of your faith. You'll become involved with both believers and non-believers. People tend to expect a great deal from religious leaders, regardless of their own beliefs. As the prospectus for the Rabbinical Diploma at the Jews' College in London warns:

'The task facing a rabbi today is a daunting one. Not only is he expected to be an authority in all areas of Jewish law, life and literature, but he is assumed to be, and criticised if he is not, a brilliant orator, a conscientious pastor, counsellor, psychologist, educationalist, politician, public relations expert, manager and leader of men.'

You'll be in contact with people from all walks of life. You can expect to share in moments of great joy at such events (depending on your particular faith) as baptisms, bar mitzvahs and weddings, as well as moments of great mental and physical suffering. At times you could be working with the dying, the destitute and those addicted to alcohol or drugs.

As a minister, you need a strong faith, compassion for others, physical and mental stamina, common sense and maturity. Religion arouses strong emotions and sometimes your efforts to help people will be met with hostility. People will challenge your beliefs.

You need to be resilient and self-reliant. Equally, you must work well with other people; much of the work of ministers is now done in teams, particularly in urban areas. Even if you don't work in a team of fellow ministers, you will probably have to collaborate with volunteers from the laity. Communication skills are vital in almost every aspect of your work from writing a parish magazine to comforting someone who is terminally ill.

'Religion is caught, not taught.'

**The Very Reverend William R Inge, former Dean of St
Paul's Cathedral**

Entry to the ministry

In addition to your spiritual and personal qualities, you may have to meet other criteria to be eligible for the ministry of your faith. In particular, note that sex discrimination laws do not apply. The Roman Catholic Church, the Orthodox Churches and Orthodox Jews only accept men into the priesthood. The Church of England has allowed women to become priests for several years, and recently appointed its first female bishop. However, there is still considerable resistance to their appointment in some areas. Reform and Liberal Jews accept women as rabbis. Celibacy and marital status are the other main issues you need to consider; you are probably aware of the stance taken in your own denomination.

Both the Church of England and Roman Catholic Church have communities of monks and nuns. Most belong to orders dedicated to a particular way of life – either to contemplation or to service through teaching, nursing and social work. Some members of holy orders are ordained priests.

Selection and training

Each faith has its own requirements and training schemes. You can get information and advice from your minister, who should be able to point you in the right direction.

Selection procedures differ, but are necessarily thorough and usually take a long time. Often you must be sponsored or 'nominated' by your parish, presbytery or bishop. Before sponsoring you they'll make sure they get to know you very well. This can take quite a long time. You'll need to talk to your parish clergy or college chaplain to start this process.

If a decision is taken to sponsor you, you are likely to be invited to an assessment centre. These are similar to those used by other employers to short-list graduates. These have different names (which appear to be constantly changing) such as a Bishops' Advisory Panel in the Church of England and an Assessment Conference in the Church of Scotland. Typically, these are residential, last two or three days, and involve about 16 people at a time. Candidates take part in group discussions and exercises as well as extended individual interviews and written exercises.

Apart from your skills and aptitudes, the assessors will be particularly concerned with your character, beliefs, motivation and vocation. As the Church of England says in its booklet *Professional Ministry*: 'The gift of faith may be something that has come to you gradually or as a sudden life-changing experience. Either way, the selector will want to know how your relationship with God is sustained and how you hope to see it grow. What place do private prayer and public worship have in your life and what experience do you have of sharing your faith with others?'

The following summarises the training programmes of some of the main faiths.

Church of England

If you're a theology graduate aged under 30 you'll undertake two years of full-time training in one of the Church's theological colleges. You may be eligible for a grant from central church funds. After ordination, most men and women start their ministry in a parish. Some remain in parishes, while others join a specialist ministry and become chaplains in industry, prisons, hospitals, universities or the Armed Forces.

Roman Catholic Church

Training to be a Roman Catholic priest normally involves six years of full-time academic study (theology and philosophy) combined with pastoral training. The length of this course is reduced if you have a theology degree. There are seminaries (theological colleges) at or near Birmingham, Durham, Guildford and London, but many ordinands (candidates for ordination) study at one of the five seminaries on the continent that accept English speaking students. After ordination most men start their ministry in a parish and may either remain in parish work or enter a specialist ministry.

Methodist Church

Training is flexible and tailored to the individual. It may be based in a residential college for two to three years. It may be through a programme of evening, weekend and summer school studies or through a combination of distance-learning and short residential courses. In all cases, biblical and theological studies, plus practical training in ministry, are the core of the programme. You're likely to become an 'Itinerant Presbyterian Minister', which means you're available to be sent anywhere in the country. Most ministers work in one place for five to ten years before being moved.

Church of Scotland

If you have taken a Bachelor of Divinity (BD) at one of the four Faculties of Divinity in Scotland, you'll undertake two years' further study. If you have a degree in another subject you'll spend at least three years studying for a BD degree. In addition you must pass three examinations, which test your knowledge of the Bible, study church law, undertake speech training and complete three six-month periods of practical work while at university. If, towards the end of your course, you are accepted as a candidate for the Church, other arrangements will be made to give you adequate practical experience. When you've passed your degree and satisfied all the other requirements you will be issued with an 'Exit Certificate'. You will then have a probationary placement of 18 months.

Orthodox Judaism

To become an Orthodox rabbi you'll have taken a three-year BA (honours) in Jewish Studies at Jews' College in London, or its academic equivalent, and studied for the three-year postgraduate Rabbinical Diploma – Semikhah. The Semikhah programme is accompanied by a regular course in Practical Rabbinics. The men joining the postgraduate course are expected to have an advanced knowledge in the study of Talmud and Halakha.

Reform or Liberal Judaism

To become a rabbi in Reform or Liberal Judaism you must first have a degree, which may be in any subject. You must then undertake a five-year, full-time course at Leo Baeck College, in London, for rabbinical ordination.

Other major religions

Other world religions are increasingly represented in Britain. The academic study of these faiths is covered in religious studies or in comparative religion (sometimes as a whole course or possibly as part of a theology degree). As a UK theology degree won't help you follow a career in these faiths, their ministries are not discussed here in detail. However, should you want to explore faiths outside the Judaeo-Christian tradition, the following notes may be helpful.

Buddhism

There are 130 Buddhist groups in Britain, as well as monasteries for monks (bhikkhus) and nuns (siladhara). Postulants (candidates) spend two years helping to run a monastery before committing themselves to the order. Once ordained, they study, teach and meditate.

Hinduism

There are 300,000 Hindus in Britain who worship in temples (mandirs). There are no training facilities for priests (pundits) in Britain. Many have studied in India or Kenya. A knowledge of Sanskrit, the language in which the Hindu texts are written, is required.

Islam

This religion has 1.6 million followers in Britain. Muslims do not have priests but imams, or prayer leaders, who are always male. Imams are appointed by their community. Formal qualifications are not needed, but a good knowledge of the Qur'an (Holy Book) is essential. The Qur'an is always read in Arabic.

Sikhism

Britain's 500,000 Sikhs worship in temples (gurdwaras). A temple committee appoints one or more granthis, or professional readers. They must understand Punjabi, the language of the Guru Granth Sahib or Holy Book.

Further information

To obtain more information about a specific faith, contact the relevant organisation below.

Baptist Church

Baptist Union of Great Britain – Ministry Office, Baptist House, 129 Broadway, Didcot, Oxfordshire OX11 8RT. Tel: 01235 517700. www.baptist.org.uk

Buddhism

The Buddhist Society – 58 Eccleston Square, London SW1V 1PH. Tel: 020 7834 5858. www.thebuddhistsociety.org

Church of England

The Vocations Officer – Ministry Division, Church House, Great Smith Street, London SW1P 3NZ. Tel: 020 7898 1399. www.cofe-ministry.org.uk

Church of Scotland

Vocational Guidance Officer – Board of Ministry, Church of Scotland, 121 George Street, Edinburgh EH2 4YN. Tel: 0131 225 5722. www.churchofscotland.org.uk

Congregational Federation

The Training Administrator – 8 Castle Gate, Nottingham NG1 7AS. Tel: 0115 911 1460. www.congregational.org.uk

Hinduism

National Hindu Students Forum UK – PO Box 46016, London W9 1WS. Tel: 07092 377 304. www.nhsf.org.uk

Islam

UK Islamic Mission – 202 North Gower Street, London NW1 2LY. Tel: 020 7387 2157. www.ukim.org

Jewish Faith (Orthodox)

United Synagogue Agency for Jewish Education – Bet Meir, 44A Albert Road, London NW4 2SJ. Tel: 020 8457 9700. www.aje.org.uk

Jewish Faith (Reform/Liberal)

Leo Baeck College – The Sternberg Centre, 80 East End Road, London N3 2SY. Tel: 020 8349 5600. www.lbc.ac.uk

Methodist Church

The Methodist Church – 25 Marylebone Road, London NW1 5JR. Tel: 020 7486 5502. www.methodist.org.uk

Roman Catholic Church (in England and Wales)

The National Office for Vocation – The Chase Centre, 114 West Heath Road, London NW3 7TX. Tel: 020 8458 6017. www.ukvocation.org

Roman Catholic Church (in Scotland)

Bishops' Conference of Scotland – 64 Aitken Street, Airdrie ML6 6LT. Tel: 01236 764061. www.scmo.org

Scottish Episcopal Church

General Synod Office – 21 Grosvenor Crescent, Edinburgh EH12 5EE. Tel: 0131 225 6357. www.scotland.anglican.org

Sikhism

Sikh Missionary Society (UK) – 10 Featherstone Road, Southall, Middlesex UB2 5AA. Tel: 020 8574 1902. www.gurmat.info

United Free Church of Scotland

General Secretary – 11 Newton Place, Glasgow G3 7PR. Tel: 0141 332 3435. www.ufcos.org.uk

United Reformed Church

Ministries Department – Church House, 86 Tavistock Place, London WC1 9RT. Tel: 020 7916 2020. www.urc.org.uk

Chapter thirteen
Careers using art and design

In the past no distinction was made between art and design. Until the end of the Renaissance, artists were in craft guilds and worked for patrons – at first the church, but then rich merchant families as well. Leonardo da Vinci, for example, was in the Goldsmiths Guild. As well as paintings he produced sculpture, military defences, machines for the textile industry and canals. He also designed elaborate sets, machinery and costumes for various festivals. Patrons usually specified the subject, the number of human figures, even the colours (pigments varied widely in price, and some patrons liked to display their wealth by choosing an expensive colour).

'There are deep affinities between art and science…both are world building: they change the shape of human culture and knowledge by adding new things to it. They do so not by mere observation but by producing material actions – experiments or works of art. The products of art and science…are designed to reveal more about the world than we knew beforehand.'

Robert P Crease, philosopher and science historian, in
Physics World

Working as an artist

Today's artists, unlike designers, are largely concerned with self-expression. Very few artists can make a living from selling original paintings or sculpture. Great talent is rarely enough. Your work must also appeal to at least some of your contemporaries or it may not sell for years. Vincent van Gogh sold only one painting in his lifetime – to his friend and fellow artist Paul Gauguin.

There are rare commissions for murals and sculptures for commercial and public buildings and spaces. Most go to well-established artists. There are also a few private commissions – very occasionally from a rich patron, but more often from people wanting portraits of people or animals. Commercial galleries accept some works to sell on commission, rarely buying them outright. Galleries display only what they believe will sell. Unsold works are eventually returned to the artist. Moreover, painters usually have to pay for good-quality framing before their works are put on display.

To sum up, it is extremely difficult to make your entire living from selling your work. You must be prepared to supplement your income in some other way.

'I paint objects as I think them, not as I see them.'

Pablo Picasso, Spanish cubist painter and sculptor

Many artists work as illustrators – producing paintings and drawings to illustrate written text. These may be for novels, textbooks or technical manuals. This type of work overlaps with that of graphic designers. Others work in the community as an artist in residence or as a community arts officer (promoting artistic activities in the locality). Such posts are often of limited duration – for example, arts centres may offer residencies lasting one or two years.

Many artists need to teach full time (part-time posts are very scarce), which means getting a postgraduate teaching qualification (see Chapter five). Some artists work as art therapists in homes for people with learning difficulties, in hospices with the terminally ill and in psychiatric hospitals. They help withdrawn patients to express themselves through painting and other forms of art. This helps to relieve patients' tensions and can provide psychiatrists with valuable clues to patients' problems from the work produced. To do this sort of work you must have a relevant postgraduate diploma. Since the introduction of state registration, art therapists, once qualified, are encouraged to continue with their professional development. Although not mandatory at present, the British Association of Art Therapists is seeking to make this a condition for renewing state registration.

'He has no talent at all, that boy. Tell him please to give up painting.'

Edouard Manet's opinion of Pierre-Auguste Renoir, both impressionist artists

Design

Artists working in design have more career opportunities, although there is still a lot of competition – especially in such popular areas as fashion design and set design. Designers must harness their artistic skills and creativity within tight constraints. They must be aware not only of the appearance of what they produce, but how well it functions, the ease and cost of production, and any other factors that may be important. Designers work under many similar constraints to Renaissance artists. You shouldn't make the mistake of thinking that designers are second-rate artists.

Design work can be categorised into two broad categories: two-dimensional and three-dimensional. Two-dimensional design is concerned with visual communication using flat surfaces, and includes graphic and textile design. Three-dimensional design concerns the design of solid shapes – from cars to jewellery, CD players to ceramics, stage sets to furniture. It may be helpful to look at some of the work you might undertake as a designer in more detail.

Two-dimensional design

As a two-dimensional designer you may work on graphic design, which includes typography (choosing and designing the layout of lettering), illustration (including photography) and the design of company symbols (logos). You may be employed by a design agency or as part of an in-house team. Organisations requiring design work on a frequent basis often have their own artists and designers. You could work freelance, but this is only advisable after some experience in employment. Areas in which graphic designers and commercial artists are employed include:

Advertising

Designing posters; advertisements for newspapers and magazines; TV, web and film commercials; product packaging; display cards etc.

Book publishing

Designing dust jackets and covers, typography, illustration (including technical illustration and photography), designing book catalogues and promotional material.

Periodical publishing

Designing covers, choosing illustrations and photographs (and sometimes creating them), typography and designing page layouts.

Multimedia publishing

Illustrating text with visual images, sound, animation, film and video clips for CD-ROMs.

Website design

Designing websites; using logic trees to help users find the information they are seeking; and illustrating text with visual images, animation and other devices.

TV, film and video

Designing opening titles, credits, animation sequences and other graphics.

Image consultancy

Designing logos and corporate 'liveries' for big organisations. This may include everything from the stationery to colour schemes for shops, offices and company vehicles.

Textile manufacturing

Designing fabrics (using patterns, colours, weaves, fibre mixtures) for garments, bedding, carpets, soft furnishings, and so on.

Three-dimensional design

You will work in one of four main areas – craft, interior, product and fashion design – each with its own specialisations.

Craft work

Craft work involves designing and producing both decorative and utilitarian items such as jewellery, silverware, handmade furniture, ceramics and glassware (including stained glass). You might work in craft workshops, designing individual, handmade or unique objects. Alternatively, you could work in craft manufacture, producing designs or prototypes for similar objects but with the intention of mass production.

Interior design

Interior design is concerned with the use, furnishing and decoration of interior spaces. Interior designers must be aware of how people use space. For example, when designing an exhibition in a museum or gallery, the designer must take into account the flow of people past the exhibits and the views they will get. They must also be aware of any safety or security aspects and of legal requirements in the design, especially in public or commercial interiors.

Interior design work falls into five main categories:

- **Consultancy** – designing interiors for ships, aircraft, hotels and other industrial, commercial and domestic buildings; also managing contracts to ensure that the work is done on time and as specified.

- **Theatre, TV and film** – designing sets; can involve historical research into details of architecture, furnishings, etc.

- **Exhibition organisers** – designing stands, usually involving collaboration with graphic designers and advertising or marketing specialists.

- **Museums** – designing gallery layout and special exhibitions.

- **Retail stores** – designing window and 'point of sale' displays.

Product design

Product design is concerned with manufactured goods such as cars, china, furniture, computers, DVD players, light fittings, mobile phones, machine tools and thousands of other products. This involves close collaboration with design engineers, production engineers and other technical specialists, as well as with marketing people who understand customer likes and dislikes. Designers in this field have to know a lot about the characteristics of materials (both in manufacturing and when the product is being used) and production methods.

Fashion design

Fashion design, which includes footwear, covers everything from haute couture to garments and shoes for mass production. Areas of employment include the following:

- **Haute couture** – fashion houses that design exclusive 'model' garments. Only one or two copies of each design are made, almost entirely by hand.

- **Wholesale couture** – similar to haute couture, but several copies of each original are made for sale through selected retail outlets.

- **Wholesale manufacturing** – designing clothes for mass production. Most designers specialise, for example, in children's garments, men's suits, sportswear, knitwear, contour fashion (swimwear, lingerie and foundation garments), shoes and so on. Designs may follow trends set by the haute couturiers or could be based on 'classic' lines. The clothes produced will range from inexpensive, seasonally changing fashion items to longer-lasting quality goods.

- **Film, TV and theatre costume design** – can involve historical research as well as design. You may be required to adapt previous costumes as well as designing completely new items.

If you want to work in design, the following words from a distinguished British engineer are apt. Although writing about civil engineering and architecture, his words apply to any design.

'What we build should always be a whole, an entity, and the job of designing it is very much the job of giving it the wholeness of a work of art, and the inevitability of the perfect tool.'

Sir Ove Arup, British engineer

Entry qualifications

No formal qualification is needed to enter art or design, only great talent. Even so, it is becoming ever more difficult to get a place unless you have a relevant degree or have undertaken a relevant vocational course. Courses vary in their entrance requirements.

Admissions tutors will expect evidence of artistic talent in a portfolio of your work.

If you intend to become an artist you should also consider taking a postgraduate teaching qualification so that you can supplement your earnings by teaching. Apart from an exceptional talent, you'll need to be resilient and flexible, and a good manager of your money (as you may have to live on a shoestring for quite a long time before your talent is properly rewarded).

To be a designer your talent must be supplemented with an ability to work in a team and a willingness, at times, to compromise your artistic standards to meet the constraints of costs, simplicity of manufacture and other factors. You'll need an interest in production techniques and in solving technical problems. You must be interested in fashion trends in their widest sense. You have to understand why people buy some products and not others.

Training and career development

As an artist you are largely responsible for your own development. You may be wise to continue taking classes and to establish contact with fellow artists.

'He [man] has what no other animal possesses, a jig-saw of faculties which alone, over three million years of life, make him creative. Every animal leaves traces of what it was; man alone leaves traces of what he created.'

Jacob Bronowski, philosopher and scientist, in
The Ascent of Man

In design, training of graduates is primarily on the job. Few employers offer formal training at any stage, although some may pay for you to attend specialist courses when you are established in your career. The Chartered Society of Designers also offers a structured programme of continuous professional development.

You are likely to start as an assistant of some kind. (Job titles are no clue whatsoever to your status, experience or responsibility. In advertising, for example, almost every designer is called an art director.) As an assistant you may initially work mainly in a supporting role, involved in routine typography, producing working drawings for a product from a designer's rough sketch, designing simple components or researching materials for someone else's interior design proposals. Further progress will depend on your performance, not only in creative terms but also as a member of a team creating a product whether it be advertising material, a knitwear design or manufactured goods.

Finding vacancies

Openings in advertising are most likely to be found in *Campaign, Marketing* and *Marketing Week*. Also check the website of the Institute of Practitioners in Advertising (IPA). Look for vacancies within publishing in *The Bookseller, Publishing News, The Guardian* (Mondays and Saturdays) and *The Independent*. Illustrators and designers should look in *The Guardian* on Saturdays, *Creative Review, Design Week* and *Design* (published by the Arts Council). Also check recruitment websites – including those of employment agencies.

Further information

The Association of Illustrators – 2nd Floor, Back Building, 150 Curtain Road, London EC2A 3AR. Tel: 020 7613 4328. www.theaoi.com

The British Association of Art Therapists – 24-27 White Lion Street, London N1 9PD. Tel: 020 7686 4216. www.baat.org

Crafts Council – 44a Pentonville Road, Islington, London N1 3BY. Tel: 020 7278 7700. www.craftscouncil.org.uk

Design Council – 34 Bow Street, London WC2E 7DL. Tel: 020 7420 5200. www.designcouncil.org.uk

Chartered Society of Designers – 5 Bermondsey Exchange, 179-181 Bermondsey Street, London SE1 3UW. Tel: 020 7357 8088. www.csd.org.uk

The Packaging Society (formed from merger of the Institute of Packaging and Institute of Materials, Minerals and Mining) – Willoughby House, 2 Broad Street, Stamford, Lincolnshire PE9 1PB. Tel: 01780 759200. www.pi2.org.uk

The British Interior Design Association (formed from merger of the Interior Designers and Decorators Association and International Interior Design Association) – 3-18 Chelsea Harbour Design Centre, Lots Road, London SW10 0XE. Tel: 020 7349 0800. www.bida.co.uk

National Society for Education in Art and Design – The Gatehouse, Corsham Court, Corsham, Wiltshire SN13 0BZ. Tel: 01249 714825. www.nsead.org

Chapter fourteen
Careers using music, drama and dance

'It is quite untrue that English people don't appreciate music.
They may not understand it but they absolutely love the noise
it makes.'

Sir Thomas Beecham, conductor

Most of us have dreamed of becoming a performer after watching
something really striking on TV or at the theatre, concert hall or
cinema. The urge is the same whether we want to act in Shakespeare
or a Harry Potter film, play the concert piano or synthesiser, sing
opera or pop, or dance in a ballet or a cruise ship cabaret.

Health warning!

Sadly, unless you have exceptional talent, together with a lot of luck,
you're unlikely to become a professional performer. And if you do,

you'll probably earn a lot less than graduates elsewhere. There are few permanent posts and many performers have to take whatever jobs they are offered. Most face regular periods of unemployment and endure financial uncertainty all their working lives. For instance, three-quarters of professional actors and actresses are out of work at any one time. There are many hopefuls and few openings.

But if you have an overwhelming compulsion to perform, really believe in your talent and are prepared to accept insecurity and living on a shoestring – go for it. You'll regret it all your life if you don't.

Qualifications

If you want to become a performer, you should insure against periods of unemployment. So get the best academic qualifications you can, and get some useful work experience to give you some transferable or key work skills (see Chapter four). It will then be easier to get temporary or part-time work when you are 'resting'.

When considering careers using music, drama or dance, you need to be aware of the limitations of degrees in these fields. University degree courses in these subjects may include a large element of performance, but they are not usually intended as a substitute for the kind of performance courses (including degree courses) offered by the specialist music, drama and dance academies. However, a university degree can equip you for careers in production, stage management, direction, and arts administration and management. You can also teach music, drama or dance in primary and secondary schools if you obtain a postgraduate teaching qualification (see Chapter five; some further details are also provided in this chapter).

This chapter covers both performance work and other career options in which you could use music, drama or dance. Where appropriate, some information has been included on alternative training for performers, so that you can see whether or not a degree will be the best route for you to follow. The information in this chapter does not follow the same pattern as in other chapters. However, you will find what you need to know to make an informed choice about which direction to take.

Studying music

University courses in music fall into two main types: the highly academic, and those that qualify you to teach music in schools, such as the BEd in music from the Faculty of Education at Cambridge.

Entry qualifications

To enter a music degree course you'll normally need two or three A levels or the equivalent, including music, plus an audition. These courses vary a lot in content and emphasis so you'll need to research them carefully. Graduate diploma courses at specialist music schools combine academic with performance training and lead to a graduate qualification. This is probably the best option if you want to perform. There are also postgraduate courses to develop performance skills for which you would probably need Associated Board Grade 8 in one instrument (or voice), and Grade 6 in a second instrument (usually piano or another keyboard instrument).

'Music creates order out of chaos; for rhythm imposes unanimity upon the divergent, melody imposes continuity upon the disjointed, and harmony imposes compatibility upon the incongruous.'

Yehudi Menuhin, violinist and conductor

Performing music

Performance work can be divided into two categories, classical and popular music, although there is a good deal of overlap between the two.

Classical music

Most classical musicians play in orchestras, ensembles or chamber groups. A minority also work as soloists. Some symphony orchestras, opera houses and smaller groups employ musicians on a full-time salaried basis. Others use freelance players who also play for other groups and work as 'session musicians' recording music for films, radio and television programmes, commercials and jingles, and backing tracks for singles and albums. Singers, similarly, may be salaried members of a professional choir, but most work freelance. There are opportunities in opera, oratorio, solo recitals and various types of concert work, which include light music and cabaret.

Hours can be long and unsociable. Most performances are given in the evenings and at weekends. Musicians also travel a lot, either to performances or while on tour in Britain or abroad. There are lengthy rehearsals and long hours of private practice if you're to retain, let alone improve, your skills. It can be quite a juggling act to fit in session work, normally held in London in the mornings.

Many freelance musicians also supplement their income by part-time private teaching.

Entry qualifications

If you aspire to becoming a concert soloist, you'll continue to undertake tuition throughout your working life. And in your practice you'll constantly strive to reach an unattainable ideal. As one of the greatest pianists of all time put it:

'I am attracted only to music which I consider to be better than it can be performed.'

Artur Schnabel, classical pianist

It is extremely hard to build up a solo career as either an instrumentalist or a singer. It's equally tough becoming a conductor and most are experienced performers. There are postgraduate courses in conducting, but these won't guarantee you a job. It's a highly competitive field.

Popular music

Professional musicians also play popular music, ranging from pop and rock, through country and western and folk, to dance music and musicals. Some combine playing an instrument, often a synthesiser or guitar, with singing. Like classical musicians, popular musicians spend their time rehearsing, performing and practising.

Many musicians work in both popular and classical music. Some performers – mainly in pop, rock and country and western – compose, write and perform their own material. Popular musicians often have to project a flamboyant personality on stage and in video recordings, and sometimes give performances that combine theatre with music.

'Music is your own experience, your thoughts, your wisdom. If you don't live it, it won't come out of your horn.'

Charlie Parker, American jazz musician

Music therapy

Music has been found to help people with physical and mental disabilities in many different ways. This has led to the appointment of music therapists working in both education and the health services. The acts of making and listening to music can help people to relax, provide them with mental stimulus and give them an emotional outlet.

To become a music therapist you must complete at least three years of full-time musical education and then take a one-year full-time (or two- or three-year part-time) postgraduate course in music therapy. The Nordoff-Robbins Music Therapy Centre at City University, Roehampton University, and the Royal Welsh College of Music and Drama run Masters degrees and postgraduate Diploma courses in music therapy, Masters degrees are also run at Anglia Ruskin University (formerly APU) and Queen Margaret University College in Edinburgh. Diploma courses are also run at Bristol University and at the Guildhall School of Music and Drama.

Music and the media

There are opportunities for radio or television producers specialising in music programmes, but you can expect to find tough competition for places. If you take a combined music and physics degree, you could become a music technologist working as a specialist sound engineer in a recording studio or in broadcasting. This, too, can be a route to becoming a producer, or it might lead into studio management (being responsible for running a studio or group of studios).

Drama

To be a professional actor, stage singer or dancer it's vital to have an Equity card. This is the membership card of the British Actors Equity Association – the trade union of the profession. Equity limits the number of new entrants to the profession, because at any one time around three-quarters of its members are unemployed.

Equity will only issue a membership card once you have produced a required number of professional contracts, or if you have graduated from a course accredited by the National Council of Drama Training (NCDT) or the Council for Dance Education and Training (CDET). If you join a full-time higher education course lasting a year or more that prepares you for a career as an actor (or as a theatre director, dancer, choreographer, singer or for a related career) you can become a student member (£15 to join, including the first year's subscription). This offers a number of benefits. Once you graduate from an accredited course you get full Equity membership without having to provide proof of work.

Contracts are difficult to obtain without an Equity card. Graduates can sometimes get into fringe and alternative theatre and build up enough experience to apply for an Equity card. However, the NCDT recommends all intending actors to complete a course of recognised training. These courses are listed in *The Official UK Guide to Drama Training* (available free from CDS, PO Box 34252, London NW5 1XJ, but include a 161mm x 228mm, stamped (54p) addressed envelope). You can also download the Guide on www.drama.ac.uk/guide.html Once you graduate from a course accredited by the NCDT or CDET, you qualify for an immediate Equity card. This allows you to apply for vacancies advertised as 'Equity only'.

It is not easy to get into an accredited drama school. Your potential is assessed by interview and audition. Auditions vary, but you must usually prepare two pieces (one Shakespeare and one modern) and perform them for the selection panel. Many schools accept only one in twenty candidates.

There are five main areas of employment for actors:

- theatre
- radio
- television
- films
- commercials.

Theatre

There are two main areas of theatre employment – touring companies and theatre companies. At one time almost every town had its own repertory theatre. These were the main learning grounds for novice actors. Today these have largely been replaced by touring companies. These perform for a few days at a time in a theatre, hall or other venue and then move on to the next. Actors may perform several plays during a tour.

Theatre companies are usually set up for one particular play or show. Shows normally run for a fixed number of weeks or months. If the show is particularly successful the run may be extended or the show may be transferred to another theatre. If the show fails, it closes early. Some actors specialise in pantomime and summer shows.

'Realism doesn't mean copying art back into life. It means making life into art: not just accepting the facts of life but elevating them.'

Sir Laurence Olivier, British actor and director

Radio

Radio uses actors in plays, poetry readings, soaps (such as *The Archers*), dramatised features, serial readings, comedy and other programmes. Most work, apart from soaps and serials, is on a one-off basis. Unlike theatre, you don't have to learn your lines but work from a script instead. On the other hand, you have only your voice with which to create characters.

Television

Actors are usually employed to work on one-off programmes, although there are opportunities in series of various lengths. TV work can be difficult to enter until you have repertory or similar broad experience. It can also be difficult competing for a part against a well-known actor.

Television directors, like film directors, record programmes in a series of short 'takes'. These rarely last more than a minute or two. Actors usually learn their lines beforehand, then rehearse each 'take' on the set and then record it at once. Scenes are often shot out of sequence. It needs skill and self-discipline on the part of the actors if characters are to develop through a story. There is also a lot of waiting time on set while equipment is prepared and technical problems are sorted out, so you must be patient. Although it's harder to develop a character than it is on the stage, the work is generally better paid and introduces the actor to a vastly bigger audience.

Film

The industry is small and opportunities are limited. Although it can take months to produce a film, most actors are hired for a few days or weeks. 'Extras' don't need to be Equity members unless they have a speaking part. The techniques used in filming are similar to those used in TV, although locations are often more exotic and the pay is better. You must be prepared to work outside the UK.

'Actors should be treated like cattle.'

Alfred Hitchcock, British-born American film director

Commercials

This can be a useful way to boost your income, but it must not be seen as a way into other areas of acting. Moreover, the work is rarely regular. Work always comes through casting agencies. TV commercials are well paid, radio less so. If you're in a fairly high-profile TV campaign, you mustn't accept work for a competing product. If you do, you're likely to lose the chance to do any future commercial work.

Dance

'Dance is the hidden language of the soul'

Martha Graham, American pioneer of modern dance

If you are considering a career in dance, you face a choice of whether to take a dance, or dance and drama degree, or to attend a specialist dance academy. In making this decision, you should be aware of the limitations of a dance or drama degree, especially as preparation for performance. While you'll dance on most dance degree courses, degree studies in the subject do not offer the extent of specialist performance training provided by the dance academies. Dance degree graduates most often enter arts administration and management, teaching, the health and leisure industry, or a completely unrelated career. Let's look at what you will need for a performance career and consider the other options for using your dancing skills.

Performance

Dancers are of two main types: ballet and modern stage. Ballet dancers may specialise in classical or contemporary ballet. Modern stage dancers cover a variety of styles. They work in light entertainment of all kinds including musicals and other stage shows, cabaret, films and television. Unless you attend a specialist school you will have no employment prospects as a ballet dancer, and few in modern stage dance.

Ballet training

To become a ballet dancer you should ideally start serious training with a professional teacher, or at a specialist school such as the Royal Ballet Lower School, at the age of 11. This means that you must have been taking basic classes from an early age. Otherwise, you will not have attained a sufficient level of competency to start specialist training. You must start full-time professional training by the time you're 16, preferably on a course accredited by the Council for Dance Education and Training (CDET). These courses last three years.

Although there are ballet schools running accredited courses throughout the country, the major ballet companies recruit their corps de ballet from their own schools. Your prospects are improved if you can attend the school of a London ballet company.

'As in the case of all branches of art, success depends in a very large measure upon individual initiative and exertion, and cannot be achieved except by dint of hard work.'

Anna Pavlova, Russian ballerina

Modern dance training

To become a modern stage dancer you don't have to be quite as dedicated or as firmly disciplined as a ballet dancer. Ideally, you should start serious training by the time you're 14, but a later start is not impossible – especially for male dancers. You would then be wise to undertake three years of training at one of the professional schools. You should choose a course that includes voice production, stagecraft, drama and singing.

Other options for dancers

Remember that any active dance career is usually quite short. Most dancers have retired from performing by the age of 40. Indeed, as ballet has become more physically demanding, most ballerinas are retiring in their mid-30s. Some, particularly those from classical ballet, may later develop osteoarthritis (inflammation of the joints) and osteoporosis (a loss of bone density leading to easily fractured bones). So you would be sensible to think about alternative careers even if you intend to spend part of your working life as a performer.

Choreography

Some dancers progress to choreography, which is creating and arranging dance. You can do this by drawing on your years of experience as a performer, or after undertaking specialist training. For example, Middlesex University runs a BA Honours Degree in

Dance Studies – Choreography Major. However, job prospects for choreographers tend to be poor, with even fewer openings than there are in performance.

Teaching dance

If you have undertaken professional training or a dance degree, you could consider teaching dance. There are certainly more openings in teaching than in performance. You might teach privately, in recreational classes, or in a professional dance school. You could teach dance as part of physical education in schools, but if you want to teach in state schools, you will need a postgraduate teaching qualification. There is more about teaching qualifications in Chapter five.

Fitness coaching

You could consider using your dance skills by coaching at a health or leisure centre. For instance, some fitness coaching uses dance in mobility or aerobic exercise. You will probably have to follow additional courses, in either health and leisure management or physical training (See Chapter nineteen).

Stage management

Stage managers and their assistants are responsible to the director for the smooth running of rehearsals and performances. They ensure that artists are in the right place at the right time. They are responsible for stage safety. They obtain props and organise lighting, sound effects, microphones, prompting and set changes. Stage managers often work in the theatre all day, and stay until the lights go out after the evening performance. The equivalent job in television is a floor manager, and in films an assistant director. There is no equivalent in radio.

There is a popular misconception that to become an assistant stage manager in the theatre is a good route to becoming an actor. Today it is not. On the other hand, a career in stage management may provide opportunities to move into directing or producing.

Directing and producing

The director is responsible for turning a script into a theatrical, film, television or radio production. Working with the producer and, where appropriate, the writer, the director is responsible for casting and is in charge of the performers, designers and technicians. The main work is in interpreting the script, working with the artists and rehearsing until the production is ready. Directors (apart from some in television companies) are usually employed by the production. A few span more than one discipline – directing drama and opera for both stage and television, for example. There is sometimes a love–hate relationship between artists and directors.

'In the theatre the director is God, but unfortunately the actors are atheists.'

Zarko Petan, Slovenian writer and director

Producers are responsible for choosing a play or commissioning a script, engaging a director and performers, financial budgeting, and for the overall shape or treatment of the production. For stage work this may also involve renting a theatre, raising money for the production and hiring the technical staff.

Other options

You could use your talent as a performer to work as an entertainments officer, perhaps at a holiday centre or on a cruise ship. Or you might enjoy organising events such as concerts and plays, doing similar work to a theatre producer. There is more on the leisure industry in Chapter nineteen.

Further information

Arts Council England – 14 Great Peter Street, London SW1 3NQ. Tel: 0845 300 6200. www.artscouncil.org.uk

Scottish Arts Council – 12 Manor Place, Edinburgh EH3 7DD. Tel: 0845 603 6000. www.scottisharts.org.uk

Arts Council of Wales – 9 Museum Place, Cardiff CF10 3NX. Tel: 029 20 376500. www.acw-ccc.org.uk

Arts Council of Northern Ireland – MacNeice House, 77 Malone Road, Belfast, Northern Ireland. Tel: 01232 385200. www.artscouncil-ni.org

Associated Board of the Royal Schools of Music – 24 Portland Place, London W1B 1LU. Tel: 0207 636 5400. www.abrsm.org

British Actors Equity Association – Guild House, Upper St Martin's Lane, London WC2 9EG. Tel: 0207 379 6000. www.equity.org.uk

Conference of Drama Schools – CDS Ltd, PO Box 34252, London NW5 1XJ. www.drama.ac.uk

Council for Dance Education and Training – Old Brewer's Yard, 17-19 Neal Street, Covent Garden, London WC2H 9UY. Tel: 020 7240 5703. www.cdet.org.uk

National Choreographers Forum – Battersea Arts Centre, Lavender Hill, London SW11 5TN. Tel: 0207 228 4990. www.danceuk.org/services/ncf.htm

National Council of Drama Training – 1-7 Woburn Walk, London WC1H 0JJ. Tel: 020 7387 3650. www.ncdt.co.uk

British Phonographic Industry (publishes a free annual guide to contemporary music education, also available on the website) – 25 Savile Row, London W1X 1AA. Tel: 020 7287 4422. www.bpi-med.co.uk

Section 3

Other careers you could consider

There are several excellent reasons why you may opt for a career that doesn't make use of your degree discipline.

You may have taken your interest in your subject as far as you wish, and choose to widen your horizons. You might even have lost interest in your subject and want to escape from it. On the other hand, you may find it impossible to find relevant work, either because your subject is non-vocational or because there aren't enough jobs in your field. Remember, the supply of arts and humanities graduates far outstrips the supply of directly relevant jobs.

Fortunately, about two-thirds of all graduate jobs that require a degree are open to graduates of any discipline. The following chapters describe the main areas of graduate employment that aren't tied to specific academic subjects. It's impossible to cover every possible opportunity, because there are thousands of types of job and few doors will be closed to you. However, the next six chapters give some idea of the major areas of choice, with Chapter twenty including some of the less obvious options.

The employers covered in this section recruit graduates for the skills they develop while studying for a degree (such as information gathering and analysis, problem solving and communication), not for their specialist knowledge. For some of these careers, particularly in financial services and some areas of management, you'll be expected to study for a recognised professional qualification during your early years at work. Although this can be equivalent to taking another degree, it's usually an excellent career investment.

In addition to the career areas described in the following section of theis book, you may also like to look at some of the career areas already described in Section 2 – in particular Chapters six, seven, eight and ten – as, whilst being related to a particular arts and humanities discipline, many of the jobs described in these chapters are also open to graduates of other disciplines.

Chapter fifteen
Careers in public service

Public administration in the UK collectively employs around three million people and offers almost every type of career. There are two broad areas of public service in the UK – the Civil Service and local government. In addition there are the various institutions of the European Union. This chapter looks at all three career areas.

Civil Service

There are more than 170 government departments and agencies that employ nearly half-a-million people in the UK. Collectively, the Civil Service is Britain's largest employer of graduates. It is responsible for a huge range of services that affect almost every area of our lives. The departments and agencies include those listed below. Their key functions are listed where these aren't obvious. Their websites are also listed.

- Crown Prosecution Service (brings criminals to trial). www.cps.gov.uk

- Department for Culture, Media and Sports. www.culture.gov.uk

- Department for Environment, Food and Rural Affairs. www.defra.gov.uk

- Department for Education and Skills. www.dfes.gov.uk

- Department for Work and Pensions. www.dwp.gov.uk

- Department of Health. www.dh.gov.uk

- Department for International Development (overseas aid/ assistance). www.dfid.gov.uk

- Department of Trade and Industry (regulates commerce, aids exports). www.dti.gov.uk

- Department for Transport. www.dft.gov.uk

- Foreign and Commonwealth Office (overseas relations). www.fco.gov.uk

- Government Communication Network (all government communication professionals). www.comms.gov.uk

- HM Revenue and Customs (assesses and collects taxes, excise duties, VAT, etc). www.hmrc.gov.uk

- HM Treasury (public revenues/expenditure and the financial system). www.hm-treasury.gov.uk

- Home Office (criminal justice, police, prison and fire services etc). www.homeoffice.gov.uk

- Lord Chancellor's Department (civil law, Supreme Court, appoints judges, etc). www.lcd.gov.uk

- Ministry of Defence. www.mod.uk

- Office of the Deputy Prime Minister (local government, housing and the regions) www.odpm.gov.uk

- Office for National Statistics (provides data on the economy). www.statistics.gov.uk

There are five broad grades in the Civil Service. These are, in order of increasing seniority:

- Administrative Assistants (basically junior clerks)

- Administrative Officers (senior clerks)

- Junior Managers (formerly called Executive Officers)

- Higher Executive and Senior Executive Officers (middle management)

- Fast Stream and Development Programme Administrators (senior management).

As you can see, administrators should not be confused with the administrative grades – the former are the most senior, the latter the most junior. It is the last three grades that offer potentially rewarding careers to graduates.

Junior Managers

These managers are responsible for putting policy into practice. You might manage a team of clerical staff, allocating and checking its work. You may have to keep abreast of changes in the law and policy, and interpret how these should be applied. You could handle specific cases, on behalf of colleagues or members of the public, where you have to make decisions based on complex law and precedent (what's been done in the past). Some working in head or regional offices don't have much to do with the public, those in local offices can have a lot of public contact. Some public contact work, such as that in the Child Support Agency, can be stressful.

Over a third of Junior Managers are in specialist posts. You may work as a tax officer, assessing people's tax, or as a tax collector. In the Department for Work and Pensions you could become an expert on a local jobs market and act as an adviser to both job seekers and employers. In the Diplomatic Service you might spend around two-thirds of your career overseas, working in embassies, high commissions or delegations. Your duties would typically include trade promotion, aid administration, consular work and personnel.

Administrators

Administrators are senior civil servants who are responsible, under government ministers, for formulating and carrying out the policy of the Government of the day. The focus of the work is on policymaking. Activities can include:

- researching and analysing policy options
- consulting and negotiating with people in other organisations
- developing systems to implement policies

- drafting replies to Parliamentary questions

- drafting new laws

- supporting ministers in departmental management.

Entry qualifications

The Civil Service is one of the largest graduate recruiters, taking about 2000 a year. Most graduates enter the Civil Service either through the 'fast stream' route (about 500 a year) or through the recruitment schemes of the individual departments or agencies. They may enter specialist grades – e.g. for accountants, linguists, information officers, librarians – or join at the same levels as non-graduates. It is worth noting that two-thirds of Civil Service recruits are aged 25 or over.

Fast-stream recruitment is aimed at those with exceptional ability and the potential to progress quickly. The main requirement is for a good honours degree (usually an upper second or a first). There are several fast-stream schemes. These include fast-streams for central departments, the Diplomatic Service, Clerkships in Parliament, Government Communications Headquarters (GCHQ), the Secret Intelligence Service (SIS) and also the European Fast Stream.

Fast-stream entrants are selected for intensive training and development to become senior managers in the Civil Service and the European Union (refer to the information on European institutions, pages 192-194 of this chapter).

The minimum academic qualification is a second-class honours degree; most successful candidates have a 2.1 or better. You'll need to be highly intelligent with good powers of analysis, sound judgement, first-class communication skills and the ability to work well with others. At selection, you won't be expected to have a detailed knowledge of the workings of government but you will be expected to show an intelligent interest in current issues and how these affect government policy.

Junior Managers don't have to be graduates but over half are. Many are chosen for their vocational skills or 'competencies' rather than their academic attainments. In either case, you need common sense and practical intelligence. You must get on with people, enjoy responsibility and be able to communicate clearly both orally and in writing.

Training and career development

Fast-stream entrants receive a mix of formal and on-the-job training in their early years of work to help them develop the required communication and management skills. Formal training in your own department is supplemented by 15 days a year at the Civil Service College. In some departments you may also be able to register for a professional accountancy qualification.

You'll undergo a testing, and closely monitored, period of probation taking in one or more carefully selected postings. You can expect to be considered for your first promotion within two to four years of joining (even faster if you are exceptionally able). You'll then have considerable responsibility. Further promotion will depend on your performance.

Junior Manager training is mostly on the job, although departments and agencies run management development courses to improve the promotion prospects of high-calibre individuals. You may be considered for professional accountancy training or other specialist training, if you show a particular aptitude. Junior Managers who've completed two or three years' service may apply to join the fast stream.

Applications

If you're interested in fast-stream entry and you're at university or college, your careers advisory service can give you a brochure and application form. The closing dates for applications are usually in late September and early January (September only for HM Revenue and Customs). If you need more information, look at the Civil Service Fast Stream Development Programme website (www.faststream.gov. uk). Your careers service can also put you in touch with one of the Civil Service Commissioners' Liaison Officers – a working civil servant who may have recently graduated from your institution.

For Junior Manager applications you should seek the advice of your graduate careers advisory service and consult the Civil Service Recruitment Gateway website (www.careers.civil-service.gov.uk). You could also look at the websites of the individual departments or agencies that interest you. Also watch for advertisements in the major annual graduate recruitment directories *Graduate Employment and Training* (GET) and *Prospects Directory*, in the graduate vacancy bulletins (*Prospects Finalist, Prospects Today* and the online *Prospects Graduate*) and in the press.

Note that the National Health Service employs its own managers, separately from the civil servants in the Department of Health. Health Service managers are employed in Regional Health Authorities and in hospitals, and are responsible for providing healthcare within a budget. As there can never be enough money to satisfy all the demands for healthcare, NHS managers invariably have difficult decisions to make. The NHS also employs accountants who work closely with their general management colleagues.

Details about the prison service are included in Chapter sixteen. For the other departments contact the individual departments. The main departments and their websites are listed at the beginning of this chapter.

Civil Service Fast Stream Development Programme – Parity (Civil Service Fast Stream), Parity House, Fleet Mill, Minley Road. Fleet, Hants GU7 9LY. Tel: 01252 776923. www.faststream.gov.uk

GCHQ – The Recruitment Office, Room A2C, GCHQ, Hubble Road, Cheltenham, Gloucestershire GL51 0EX. Tel: 01242 709095/6. www.gchq.gov.uk

Health and Safety Executive – Magdalen House, Trinity Road, Bootle, Merseyside L20 3QZ. Tel: 0845 345 0055. www.hse.gov.uk

National Health Service Management Training Schemes

NHS Management Training Schemes (England) – Innovation Court, New Street, Basingstoke RG21 7JB. Tel: 01325 745818. www.futureleaders.nhs.uk

NHS Management Training Schemes (Scotland) – HR Department, NHS National Services Scotland, Gyle Square, 1 South Gyle Crescent, Edinburgh EH9 12EB. Tel: 0131 244 3451. www.managementtrainingscheme.nhsscotland.com

NHS Management Training Schemes (Wales) – National Leadership and Innovation Agency for Healthcare, Innovation House, Bridgend Road, Llanharan CF72 9RP. Tel: 01443 233333. www.nliah.wales.nhs.uk

NHS Management Training Schemes (Northern Ireland) – The Beeches Management Centre, 12 Hampton Manor Drive, Belfast BT7 3EN. Tel: 028 9064 4811. www.beeches-mc.co.uk

Local government

Local government is concerned with providing services to the community. In career terms, it is a group of several hundred employers throughout Great Britain. Collectively they employ about two-and-a-half million people.

Few people realise just how wide a range of services is provided by local government authorities. These include:

- education

- environmental health

- fire service

- highways (building and repairs, traffic management, street lights, pavements, snow clearing)

- housing

- libraries

- police

- promoting tourism

- public conveniences

- recreation, arts and museums

- social services

- strategic and local planning, and all planning applications

- trading standards (consumer protection)

- transport

- waste collection and disposal.

In England there are two levels (or 'tiers') of local government – county councils and district councils in the non-metropolitan areas, and unitary (i.e. single tier) authorities in metropolitan and London Borough Councils. There are unitary authorities throughout Scotland and Wales. County councils provide the large-scale strategic services such as education and highways. Unitary authorities provide all local government services.

As you'll realise from looking at the list of services above, there's a huge range of career opportunities available. A number of these are professional careers. Many can be followed both inside and outside local government. These include accountancy and finance, archive work, IT, librarianship, museum work and public relations. For others, such as the police, local government is the major or only employer. These are discussed in other chapters.

Local government also employs many people in administrative roles, for example, managers who hold senior departmental posts. They provide support to council committees and subcommittees, advise councillors, and research and prepare reports, sometimes involving the compilation and analysis of statistical information. You do not have to have a degree to enter administrative grades, but it is very useful.

Training is primarily on the job, although you will be encouraged to undertake further study (perhaps by day-release or correspondence course) for instance to qualify for membership of the Institute of Chartered Secretaries and Administrators (ICSA).

Because each authority is an individual employer, conditions of employment and training schemes differ between authorities. Salaries also vary according to the size and type of authority. However, local authorities generally have a good reputation regarding their conditions of employment and commitment to the training and development of their people. They often provide day-release or part-time study for job-related qualifications. They also actively encourage staff to qualify for membership of a relevant professional body.

Promotion opportunities at senior level may be restricted within a single authority. Career advancement is commonly made by moving from one local authority to another. Although this involves applying to openly advertised posts, preference is usually given to people who already work in local government and so have relevant experience.

The Employers' Organisation for local government runs a National Graduate Development Programme, which aims to recruit and develop senior managers and chief executives of the future. There are four elements to this programme: core placements within a 'host' local authority, studying for a Postgraduate Diploma in Local Government Management (PGDLGM); national training; and external mentoring. www.lgcareers.com/getting/grad.htm

Some councils run their own graduate training schemes. You can get information on these from their human resources departments. Councils also recruit graduates into particular jobs in many different occupational areas such as planning, legal work, accountancy, IT, personnel, marketing, policy and research. For details of current job vacancies in local councils check www.lgjobs.com

Finding vacancies

Local Government Opportunities (LGO) provides vacancy information on the internet (www.lgcareers.com). Otherwise, you should look out for advertisements for specific vacancies. You will find these in *The Guardian* (Wednesdays), *Opportunities: The Public Sector Recruitment Weekly* (Fridays; see also the website www.opportunities.co.uk) as well as in relevant professional and trade journals.

The European institutions

The European Commission and other institutions of the European Union are having an ever-increasing impact on life in the UK and other member countries. Moreover, the EU has recently admitted several new members from Eastern Europe and a number of other countries are seeking membership. Although the institutions recruit their staff from throughout the Union, Britain is not well represented. The British Government and the various institutions themselves are keen to improve the situation.

The European institutions, with their main functions, are:

■ **The European Commission** – proposes all legislation; ensures legislation is implemented; represents the community internationally

■ **The Council of the European Union** – composed of ministers from each member state; adopts EU legislation

■ **The European Parliament** – proposes changes to legislation; has the last word on aspects of the budget; and has the power to dismiss the Commission

■ **The Court of Justice** – rules on the interpretation and application of EU law

■ **The Court of Auditors** – supervises the Union's budget.

As from 1 May 2006, graduates will be recruited into AD grade and non-graduates into AST grade. Each grade is subdivided into numerical levels, with 1 being the most senior. Your degree must be at a level that would qualify you for entry to doctoral studies. All categories of staff are recruited through competitive exams, known as 'open competitions', which are held whenever the EU needs to recruit staff with particular skills and qualifications. Some competitions are open to graduates of any discipline, while others may require a specific subject such as law or economics.

Selection procedures

The European institutions use a recruitment system that is totally alien to British candidates and is a main reason why so few Britons work for them. Speculative applications are not accepted. The 'open competitions' (see below) are announced in the national press (usually *The Times, The Independent, Financial Times* and *The Guardian*) and are fully described in *The Official Journal of the European Communities*. See website at www.europa.eu.int/epso/index_en.htm

If you are accepted as eligible, you usually face three stages of selection: multiple-choice preselection tests, written tests and oral tests – and you must pass each stage before you go onto the next. Your knowledge of your stated languages will also be tested.

To help British AD grade candidates, a 'European Fast Stream' recruitment scheme has been introduced (see the information on the Civil Service, earlier in this chapter). If you're accepted for this scheme, you are employed as a 'fast track' trainee in the Civil Service, but with the intention of entering the competitions for vacancies in the European institutions. You will prepare for the European recruitment competitions through a combination of relevant work experience and training. Even this scheme can't guarantee success in finding a post in the European institutions, but you will be able to remain in the UK Civil Service if you don't succeed.

Entry qualifications

If you apply to the European Fast Stream the entry qualifications are the same as for the UK Fast Stream programme, except that you must also show an awareness of EU affairs and some understanding of how the institutions work. You'll also need a working knowledge of two European languages in addition to your own.

Training and development on the Fast Stream is also very similar to that for the UK Fast Stream, but it will include some additional elements to coach you for the competitions, develop your language skills and to help prepare you for working in Europe. Your postings, which are likely to include temporary attachments to Brussels and Luxembourg, will be carefully chosen to give you experience of European questions. If you do join a European institution you'll have to resign from the Civil Service. However, you retain the right to return to the UK Civil Service within five years.

Further information

Literature, advice for telephone and written enquiries, a website and a vacancy information service is provided by :

The European Union Staffing Team – Room 61A/2 , Cabinet Office, Horse Guards Road, London SW1P 3AL. Tel: 020 7270 6138. www.euro-staff.gov.uk

Europa, The European Union On-Line – Detailed information on the European Union (including recruitment policies). www.europa.eu.int

Rebecca Swainson

Rebecca, 27, is a personal adviser with the Connexions service in Wiltshire and Swindon. Her employer, Lifetime Careers Wiltshire, is contracted to deliver part of the Connexions service in that area. Increasingly, people working in the public services are employed by private companies which deliver services under contract to local and national Government bodies.

Career profile

Job title: personal adviser

Employer: Lifetime Careers Wiltshire

A levels: English literature, history and communication studies

Degree: BA English literature

University: De Montfort University, Leicester

Postgraduate qualification: Diploma in Careers Guidance, University of West of England in Bristol

'I chose my degree subject of English literature because it was what I was best at doing and a subject I'd loved since GCSE. And I chose Leicester because it seemed a lively student town, inexpensive to live in and far enough from home but not too far away.

I enjoyed most of my degree course, although I found you have to work far more independently than I expected. There were also lots of modules offered on the English honours degree, so I had a lot of choice, but I was never with the same group of people. So I never got to bond with classmates to the extent I wanted. There wasn't that much class contact, especially in my third year when I was doing my dissertation. I had four to six hours of class contact a week – the rest of the time was spent working in the library and studying on my own. You had to learn to be very self-directing in your study.

In my second year I got involved in some volunteering. I was interested in social care and counselling related jobs and started unpaid voluntary work for the Leicester Education Action Zone. We went into secondary school classrooms to act as mentors to young people, or assist in the classroom. It is quite challenging in city schools – but an eye opener – dealing with the needs of the children and behaviour issues. But I did enjoy it, and found it personally rewarding when I had really helped someone and they appreciated the time I had given them.

I was lucky and could manage my money, so I didn't need a part-time job during term-time. But I did various summer vacation jobs. I worked for BT directory enquiries for two summers – giving out phone numbers. I also worked as a post woman

– very early starts, sorting and delivering the post.

I really started considering what I wanted to do early in my third year. I thought I wanted to teach, but my experiences in the classroom put me off. So I started thinking about what other roles there are in education supporting young people. I did some research and discovered the careers service – which was being rebranded into 'Connexions'.

I went to the university careers service, and they said that to get a careers guidance qualification you need postgraduate training. The nearest course to me was a Postgraduate Diploma in careers guidance at the University of the West of England in Bristol. I applied and was accepted. This one-year course gave me two qualifications: the Postgraduate Diploma in careers guidance, awarded by the university; and the Qualification in Careers Guidance awarded by a professional body, The Institute of Careers Guidance.

Just before the course finished I started looking for a job, applying to various Connexions services for posts they had advertised. I finished my course in June, and found a job with Lifetime Careers, one of the partners involved in delivering Connexions in the Swindon and Wiltshire area.

I like it, but it's a bit different from what I imagined – for example, I found that gathering statistics was something I don't much enjoy. But Connexions is quite a targeted service, so we are working with vulnerable young people who may be disaffected or disengaged from learning. So I enjoy the challenge of trying to find out what their issues are, what their barriers to learning might be and looking at ways in which I can help them to move forward.

At the moment I'm still a probationer doing work-based training. I would like to get involved in more in-depth work within the service. Some of our more experienced advisers work in more specialist roles such as helping young people with special needs.

That's something I'd quite like to do.

If you take an arts or humanities degree, say English or history, it helps you to keep your options open for longer. You are still developing skills in research, analysis and problem solving. But it is not specific vocational training. So you need to be able to articulate those skills to employers. You need also to look at other ways in which you can enhance your degree by perhaps doing something like voluntary work, part-time jobs, an internship or even doing a sandwich course.'

Chapter sixteen
Careers in the uniformed services

The major uniformed professions are the Armed Forces, the police, nursing, and the fire, ambulance, security and prison services. Although they cover a range of very different activities, they have some things in common:

- they provide a public service, and often undertake tasks that most people wouldn't want to do

- the work can sometimes expose them to danger

- they must obey more rules and regulations than most civilians

- there's a lot of discipline – imposed discipline and self-discipline

- they work unsocial hours.

The nature of the work, the shared risks, the discipline and the irregular hours tend to separate members of the uniformed services from the general population. Each service has a strong esprit de corps.

The nursing profession and the fire and rescue, ambulance and security services do not have graduate entry schemes, so your degree will give you little or no advantage (although you can take a degree in nursing, and graduates of other disciplines may follow a shortened course of training at some schools of nursing). However, you may well find the work very satisfying, and worth considering for that reason alone. Most of the other services do have 'fast track' or similar schemes for graduates and it is on those services that this chapter is focused.

Armed Forces officers

The main purpose of the Armed Forces is to defend our country and to help allies to whom we are bound by treaty. They are also involved in peacekeeping missions and disaster relief. Relations between the major nations have improved, thus allowing cuts in defence spending. However, the world is very far from conflict free and there are constant threats from terrorism. Recent cuts in defence expenditure, combined with the growing demands made on our Armed Forces, means that they must now sometimes work with insufficient people and inadequate equipment.

Most officers have two roles: to lead and manage a team of people, and to be a technical specialist. The balance between the two roles varies by rank and by the service you're in. The responsibility of a Pilot Officer in the RAF is primarily as a specialist, whereas that of a Second Lieutenant leading an infantry platoon in the Army is mainly leadership and management. However, as each rises through the ranks, each assumes greater responsibility for both roles.

Some people who join the Armed Forces in peacetime assume that they won't be called upon to share the risks or responsibilities that are expected of them in times of war. This is not the case. Conflicts can arise unexpectedly, as in Afghanistan and Iraq. Servicemen and women must be prepared to risk their lives at any time, whether defending our country and its interests, acting as international peacekeepers, or during disaster relief.

You need to face the moral question – would you be prepared to kill or order the killing of other human beings?

A recruitment brochure for Army officers reminded applicants that in defending one way of life:

> 'It could be your duty to give an order to fire – and not necessarily in a battle where the enemy is identifiable, but possibly against terrorists of one sort or another who are not wearing uniforms and who are doing their best to fight behind the cover of the civilian population. Not everyone would be prepared to give that order, justify their actions, and take the responsibility...'

The Armed Forces offer a huge range of career opportunities for specialists. For example, because modern defence and warfare systems use a lot of sophisticated technology, some roles require graduate engineers. The Armed Forces also require qualified professionals such as lawyers, doctors and dentists. Equally, there are also plenty of openings for arts and humanities graduates as officers. Let's look at the options in each of the Forces in turn.

Army

> 'An army of asses led by a lion is better than an army of lions led by an ass.'

> **George Washington, first President of the USA**

Listed below are the areas (with an indication of their role within the Army) in which there are openings suitable for arts and humanities graduates:

- **Royal Armoured Corps** – armoured regiments, which are equipped with main battle tanks and armoured reconnaissance regiments using fast reconnaissance vehicles

- **Royal Regiment of Artillery** – the Army's largest single regiment, provides ground fire support and air defence using a range of guns and surface-to-surface and surface-to-air missiles

- **Infantry** – this represents a quarter of the Army, and includes the parachute regiment; the Infantry bears the brunt of fighting on the ground using a variety of weapons

- **Special Air Service Regiment** – has responsibility for special operations (the SAS is open only to those who have proved themselves elsewhere in the Army)

- **Army Air Corps** – operates all Army helicopters – used for missile attacks, troop carrying, reconnaissance and as airborne command posts

- **Intelligence Corps** – collects, collates and analyses information on the enemy and combats espionage, subversion and sabotage

- **Royal Logistic Corps** – stocks and distributes stores and equipment; handles all catering and food supplies; transports people and freight; has responsibility for bomb disposal

- **Royal Corps of Signals** – maintains the Army's command, control and information systems; provides secure communications and provides worldwide satellite communications

- **Adjutant General's Corps** – has four branches, one providing all personnel administration for the Army, another providing educational and training services.

Royal Navy

Entrants can specialise as officers in the following areas:

- **Warfare Officer** – commands ships at sea; controls the ship's weapon systems and coordinates air, submarine and surface unit attacks

- **Air Traffic Control** – airspace control of wide variety of high performance aircraft

- **Aircrew** – observers and pilots of helicopters

- **Submarine Warfare Officer** – nuclear Fleet submarines are used for defence against enemy surface ships and submarines, and intercontinental ballistic missile submarines; open only to men

- **Logistics** – ensures that a ship has all the equipment, accommodation, food, supplies and manpower it needs and also provides advice on personnel, legal and accountancy topics

- **Royal Marines** – the Royal Navy's commandos; includes an elite group, the Special Boat Service (SBS), who are the waterborne equivalent of the SAS.

Royal Air Force

Officers in the Royal Air Force (RAF) may work as one of the following:

- **Pilot** – flies many different types of aircraft such as fighters, transport aircraft and helicopters

- **Navigator** – works with pilots to control aircraft systems, plan and monitor routes, watch for enemy, coordinate evasive action, etc

- **Air traffic controller** – helps aircraft take off, land and move through the area they are responsible for; works closely with civil air traffic control

- **Fighter controller** – uses data from radar and other systems to monitor airspace and to direct fighters to intercept aircraft

- **Provost** – the RAF's police force: responsible for all aspects of security and investigating criminal offences on or around air stations

- **The RAF Regiment** – defending RAF airfields and installations against ground and low-level air attack

- **Supply** – providing equipment and supplies from an inventory of 1.6 million different items; transports cargo/personnel by air, road, rail and sea

- **Intelligence** – gathering/interpreting information using stereoscopic, panchromatic or infra-red photography or electro-optical imaging.

Entry qualifications to the Armed Forces

Any subject is accepted – although for the Royal Corps of Signals and for RAF pilots, navigators and intelligence officers, a science or technology degree is an asset. Graduates with a language degree are welcomed in the Royal Corps of Signals and the Intelligence Corps. As well as your degree, personal qualities are important. Although it is a remarkably diverse group of people who become officers (or 'earn the Queen's Commission'), they do share some qualities. They're good problem solvers and have plenty of common sense. Contrary to popular belief, officers must have minds of their own and be able to stand up for themselves. They can think on their feet and make quick decisions. They can express themselves easily and clearly. They're physically fit and have plenty of stamina. Perhaps most importantly, they have leadership skills and can motivate and encourage others by their personal example.

Officer selection

Recruitment takes place via selection boards. These combine practical initiative tests, group exercises, written aptitude tests, discussions with fellow applicants, and interviews. Procedures vary a little from service to service. The process is rigorous and probably the fairest selection method yet devised. Many graduate employers in other fields now use similar methods under the name of 'assessment centres'. The individual boards are:

- **The Regular Commissions Board** – selection tests for the Army, which take place at Westbury in Wiltshire, and last three days

- **Admiralty Interview Board** – selection tests for the Royal Navy, held at HMS Sultan at Gosport, which last two days

- **Officers and Aircrew Selection Centre** – holds tests for entrance to the Royal Air Force, which last three days, at Cranwell in Lincolnshire.

Training and career development

This varies from service to service and also according to your specialisation. The following is only a brief outline.

Army

You join the Army as an officer cadet and attend a Commissioning Course at the Royal Military Academy at Sandhurst in Surrey. This lasts 11 months and consists of three terms, each lasting 14 weeks interspersed with a period of leave and one week's adventure training. When you 'pass out' from Sandhurst your commission will be confirmed. You'll then undergo further training to prepare you for your regiment or corps. You'll get back-dated promotion for the years you spent studying for your degree, so you'll be paid as a Lieutenant instead of a Second Lieutenant. Army life is made up of 'tours' normally lasting two years. Your first will be with a regiment or corps.

You'll undergo further training at all stages of your career. In a full Army career, you could spend the equivalent of six or seven years on courses. Throughout your career you'll move between two career paths – regimental duty, where you develop your leadership and man management skills, and staff work, where you develop other managerial and administrative skills.

Royal Navy

All entrants join on an 'initial' 12-year commission (eight-year for the Royal Marines). You are then eligible for competitive selection to a 'career' commission (service through to 16 years from the age of 21 and above). Similarly, you may be selected for a 'full-term' commission that will take you to the age of 55.

You will undertake 28-49 weeks of training (depending on your specialisation) at the Britannia Royal Naval College at Dartmouth in Devon. The practical stage of this training is spent with the Dartmouth Training Squadron. You'll travel abroad and gain valuable experience working with ship's ratings (the lower non-commissioned ranks). Finally, you will undergo Fleet training in anything from a destroyer to a minesweeper. During Fleet training you'll spend up to nine months studying for your Fleet Board Examination while carrying out watchkeeping duties and working in each of the specialist departments. You can expect to move every two or three years through a variety of different posts to broaden your experience.

'The Royal Navy of England hath ever been its greatest defence and ornament, it is its ancient and natural strength; the floating bulwark of the island.'

William Blackstone, 18th-century English jurist

Royal Air Force

Your RAF training starts with a 24-week Initial Officer Training Course at the RAF College at Cranwell in Lincolnshire. You then undertake professional training in your particular branch. Pilots attend Elementary Flying Training at Linton-on-Ouse. During this course, you will be streamed according to your suitability for fast jet, helicopter or multi-engined aircraft flying, and will then undertake further training. Navigators begin their professional training at RAF Cranwell and are then streamed, like the pilots, according to aircraft group. Each of the other specialist areas provides its own professional training.

Promotion prospects

Promotion is usually automatic (subject to your annual confidential reports and passing promotion examinations) up to the level of Captain in the Army, Lieutenant Commander in the RN, and Flight Lieutenant in the RAF. Beyond these levels, selection is competitive.

Applications

If you are still at school you should (through your careers teacher) contact the Schools Liaison Officer of the service that interests you. It is worth doing this because the Forces provide scholarships for selected students through their last two years (aged 16-18) at school. They may also be able to arrange an 'acquaint visit' so that you can experience something of service life.

There are also schemes to sponsor those who wish to become officers through their university course. You should apply as soon as you have a confirmed university place. If you are already at university, you should contact the Graduate Liaison Officer through your careers service.

If you're interested in a period in the Armed Forces, but don't want to make it a lifelong career, the services offer short-service commissions. These vary in length by service. They range from a minimum three years (Army and RAF) to a minimum eight years in the Royal Navy. The Army also offers a 'gap' year limited commission. If you undertake a short-service commission you will learn a range of skills that are directly transferable to a management career in civilian life. Employers generally welcome people with service experience because of their self-discipline and leadership qualities.

Further information

You can get more details and copies of up-to-date literature on graduate careers from your local Armed Forces Careers Office. You can also check their individual websites or order an information pack.

Army Officer Entry – Tel: 0845 7300111. www.army.mod.uk

RAF Officer Careers – Tel: 0845 605 555. www.rafcareers.com

Royal Navy and Royal Marines – Tel: 0845 607 5555. www.royal-navy.mod.uk and www.royal-marines.mod.uk

The police

Britain does not have a national police force, but 52 separate forces (43 in England and Wales, eight in Scotland and one in Northern Ireland). However the Government is discussing the possibility of merging several forces. Their role is to protect life and property, and to enforce law and order. However, they have no part in creating the laws or in deciding the punishment given out to offenders.

'The purpose of the police service is to uphold the law fairly and firmly; to prevent crime; to pursue and bring to justice those who break the law; to keep The Queen's Peace; to protect, help and reassure the community; and to be seen to do this with integrity, common sense and sound judgement.'

Extract from 'The Statement of Common Purpose and Values'

Members of the public don't fully understand the difficulties of police work, or the extent of the tasks that we have given them through our Members of Parliament. We sometimes expect more than the police can deliver. Some members of the public can be uncooperative and even hostile.

'When constabulary duty's to be done, the policeman's lot is not a happy one.'

Sir W S Gilbert, librettist and playwright

After completing their training, all entrants start work as uniformed constables on the beat. The work includes helping members of the public and answering queries, checking the security of premises, apprehending and interviewing suspects, investigating crimes and taking statements from witnesses, and dealing with accidents, disturbances and traffic problems. Not all their time is spent on foot or car patrol. There's a lot of paperwork and some time is spent in court. Later, you can specialise in such areas as:

- the Criminal Investigation Department (CID), which investigates serious crimes

- the traffic department, which promotes road safety, controls traffic flow, and deals with traffic accidents and offences

- the river police service, which patrols rivers and coastal waters to prevent theft and smuggling, and performs life saving.

Promotion is through the ranks, with sergeants supervising the work of police constables. Inspectors divide their time between operational and management roles. As you progress through the senior ranks, you take on managerial roles of increasing importance. The more senior you become, the more you will be involved in liaising with the leaders of the community you serve.

Entry qualifications

Every candidate applies for entry to a specific force. As a graduate, as soon as you get a job offer from your chosen force, you can apply to the High Potential Development scheme (HPD) whatever your discipline. Although the scheme is also open to non-graduates, if you don't have a degree you must study for one as a mandatory part of the programme. Graduates can also study for a higher degree. You need to be physically fit, and there are minimum eyesight standards that vary from force to force.

The selection process is rigorous. You must first be accepted as a police constable in the force to which you have applied. The HPDS selection procedure is in the form of an assessment centre taking about three days (two or three days in Scotland). You will have to tackle a mixture of interviews, individual aptitude tests and group exercises. Your interviewers assess your 'all round intellectual, personal and professional abilities'. Among the qualities sought are self-discipline and the ability to understand complex material, deal with unexpected problems and learn from limited experience. You must also have good oral and written communication skills. You need mental as well as physical stamina. Perhaps above all, your interviewers need to be satisfied that you really want to become a police officer.

Training and career development

At present those who are selected for the High Potential Development (HPD) scheme undertake a two-year probationer course that involves formal classroom training, going on patrol with a tutor and then without, and attending a variety of mainly optional training courses. However, the probationer programme is expected to change very soon.

Currently, you would be assessed every six months through a performance development review. You would be expected to contribute to this assessment as it is used for identifying your development needs. It is also used to assess you for promotion. Those on the scheme are not subject to the usual promotion procedures of their local police force. You can remain on the scheme until you reach superintendent level.

Applications

Before you apply to the police you want to be sure it's right for you. Most forces run familiarisation courses each autumn. These usually include spending three or four days on patrol with officers. You can get application forms and details of closing dates from the Graduate Liaison Officer.

You apply for entry to your chosen police force, and once you have been offered a job, you then apply to the High Potential Development Scheme. You can find out more on the website www.policehighpotential. org.uk and you will find a list of all UK police forces (except Scotland) on the internet at www.policecouldyou.co.uk (Scottish police forces are listed at www.scottish.police.uk).

The Police Graduate Liaison Officer – Room 553, Home Office, Queen Anne's Gate, London SW1H 9AT. Tel: 08456 083000 (quote HPD Scheme). www.homeoffice.gov.uk

The HPD HQ – HPD Scheme Office, 4th Floor Fry, 2 Marsham Street, London SW1P 4DF. Tel: 020 7035 5050. www.policehighpotential.org.uk

The Accelerated Promotion Coordinator (for Scotland) – The Scottish Police College, Tulliallan Castle, Kincardine, Alloa, Clackmannanshire FK10 4BE. Tel: 01259 732000. www.tulliallan.police.uk

Prison Service

HM Prison Service has to look after people who are committed to its care by the courts. It operates about 130 institutions in England and Wales. There are also 11 privately-run prisons. In Scotland, the Scottish Prison Service operates 15 prisons. As well as offenders of all ages, including juveniles, who have been sentenced to various terms of imprisonment, there are also remand prisoners still awaiting either trial or sentencing by the courts following conviction.

To do this doesn't simply involve keeping prisoners locked up, fed and exercised. It also requires officers to care for the physical and mental health of their charges, advising and helping them with their personal problems, offering education and training, and providing work experience. The aim isn't only to control prisoners but also to provide them with as full a life as possible and to rehabilitate them, so that they might return to the outside world as law-abiding citizens.

'Her Majesty's Prison Service serves the public by keeping in custody those committed by the courts. Our duty is to look after them with humanity and help them lead law-abiding and useful lives in custody and after release.'

Prison Service, 'Statement of purpose'

The work of a prison officer is frustrating at times. The service often fails in its aim to rehabilitate prisoners, most of who re-offend after release. Some prisoners are abusive, and a few are violent. Many prisons are old and overcrowded, although there is an ongoing programme of new building and refurbishment. Prisoners often suffer from feelings of anxiety, anger and depression. Many worry about their families and often feel totally helpless if there are problems at home. Unless prison staff spot and deal with these emotional problems, tensions can build up and sometimes erupt in rioting.

In spite of the negative aspects, the work provides many opportunities to help others who are in unfortunate circumstances. It also offers a range of management challenges. These aspects of the job can be highly satisfying.

Entry qualifications and selection procedure

For general entry to the service there are no specific academic requirements, but the Intensive Development Scheme is aimed exclusively at graduates. At present there is no accelerated promotion scheme in Scotland.

You must have the potential to lead and motivate others – both colleagues and prisoners. You must have the assertiveness to enforce discipline while being neither aggressive nor authoritarian. You need persuasive communication skills. You will have to make difficult decisions when necessary and be capable of explaining them clearly.

There is a three-stage selection process. Firstly, you will complete a 'Core Management Skills Assessment Form' as part of your initial application. If you pass this stage you attend a one-day assessment centre undergoing written exercises to assess your analytical skills, decision making and problem solving. Finally, if successful you will attend a two-day assessment centre that looks at your interpersonal skills.

The Prison Service also directly recruits staff into a wide range of more senior management posts including procurement (buying), accountancy and personnel.

Training and career development

Those on the Intensive Development Scheme will firstly complete full training to become a prison officer, followed by up to 12 months carrying out the full range of prison officer duties. You would then progress to senior officer with responsibility for a group of staff. Your next move would be to trainee operational manager (a middle-management governor position). Your rate of progress is determined by your performance.

At each stage you will sit the key assessment centres and will be supported by the Leadership and Management Development programme with both on- and off-the-job mentors, and a dedicated training programme. Within two-and-a-half to three years of joining the scheme you could be head of a busy unit, or function, within a prison. Your further progress will be up to you.

Applications

Vacancies on the Accelerated Promotion Scheme in England and Wales are advertised in the national press during September, with a closing date at the end of November, to start the following September. An information pack and application form is available from the address below.

Management Selection and Succession Unit – Prison Service HQ, Room 328-9, Cleland House, Page Street, London SW1P 4LN. Tel: 020 7217 6437. www.liveslessordinary.co.uk

Information on prison careers in Scotland is available from:

Scottish Prison Service – Central Recruitment Board, Calton House, 5 Redheughs Rigg, Edinburgh EH12 9HW. Tel: 0131 244 8745. www.sps.gov.uk

Chapter seventeen
Careers in management

In the past, the traditional graduate career took you into a profession, the Civil Service or into management. Those entering management usually joined a large organisation – such as Shell, Unilever, HSBC or PricewaterhouseCoopers – as a management trainee. After a year or two on a formal training scheme, you progressed up the promotional ladder into senior management. But what is management? What do managers do? Is the traditional traineeship still the normal route into management? Do you still progress in the same way? In this chapter we'll look at the basic role of management in business, describe some of the management functions in which you could make a career, look at the entry routes and discuss career progression.

What is management?

Although we all know the word 'manager', there is no clear definition of what a manager is or does. There are probably as many definitions of management as there are businesses. And there is no general agreement on what qualities make a good manager. The problem is that there are many kinds of management job, and they're carried out in many different ways. Moreover, not everyone called a 'manager' is one. Some are given the title to make them appear more important to an organisation's customers. For example, some businesses call every sales person a 'sales manager'. On the other hand, there are some management jobs that do not have 'manager' in the job title – such as an orchestral conductor, the leader of a Himalayan climbing expedition, or a commissioned officer in the Armed Forces.

A manager is responsible for running an enterprise, or section of an enterprise, and safeguarding its future. Whether you are managing a manufacturing firm, a government or local government department or a services company, the principles are the same. You must develop products or services that satisfy your customers' needs at an affordable price and ensure they are available when and where they are needed. As public service is covered in Chapter fifteen, this chapter concentrates on business organisations.

'Business underlies everything in our national life, including our spiritual life. Witness the fact that in the Lord's Prayer the first petition is for daily bread. No one can worship God or love his neighbour on an empty stomach.'

Thomas Woodrow Wilson, 28th president of the USA

Whatever field they are in, the work of managers can be broken down under six main headings. Firstly, they set their team's objectives. Then they must organise, by working out what needs to be done and allocating people to these tasks. Thirdly, they must communicate lucidly so that each person understands what the enterprise is trying to achieve and what they are personally responsible for. They must also motivate each person in the team to give their willing effort. They must set targets for their team. And finally, they must develop the knowledge and skills of the individuals in their team.

The principles are the same whatever your business. You could work in a forestry company growing timber or a quarrying group producing crushed stone for railway ballast and road surfacing. You may manufacture jewellery or jet aircraft, books or baby clothes, cars or confectionery. Or you may provide accommodation and meals through a hotel, sell food and goods in a supermarket, provide transport through an airline or bus company, sell houses through an estate agency, or provide entertainment through a theatre, disco or concert hall.

Different management functions

To run any business, especially a large and complex business, involves a wide range of specialist management functions. It's worth looking at the main ones.

Product development

This concerns creating new or improved products. If you're in business to make such things as space satellites, packaged foods, pharmaceuticals, computers or toiletries, you will have research and development teams of scientists and technologists. If your products are items such as fabrics, china, furniture, clothing or jewellery then designers will create these. The team must liaise with marketing, in order to design products that meet customer needs, and with production, to ensure that the designs are practical to make.

Marketing

Marketing is central to the business. Marketing people work closely with every other function. They identify markets for existing and new products. They might suggest ideas for new products that need to be developed. They investigate potential new markets and existing markets to find out what new products could be introduced. The team will either conduct or commission market research. They work with specialists to create an identity or 'image' for the product through carefully thought out brand names, packaging, advertising and other promotional campaigns. They watch what their competitors are doing and monitor the performance of products in terms of sales, customer satisfaction and profitability against theirs.

Nathan Webb

Nathan, 23, has managed to combine his interest in the theatre with a career in marketing.

Career profile

Job title: marketing assistant

Employer: Marlowe Theatre, Canterbury

A levels: history, German, theatre studies

Degree: BA theatre and performance

University: Warwick

'When I was at school I had no particular idea of what I hoped to do eventually, though for a long time I was into performing on stage – acting and that sort of thing. And then when I was doing my A levels I got interested in directing. I did a couple of shows, as a director, with a youth theatre group in Frome. I also worked at the box office of the Merlin Theatre in Frome and did a few extra shifts in the marketing department there. I guess I always assumed that I would end up working in some capacity in theatre, the arts or somewhere like that. But I didn't have any specific plans at school.

My choice of degree subject was dictated by my interest and wanting to know more about theatre. A large part of my degree was contemporary performance practice – more performance art – and I got quite into that at university.

A lot of the degree I did was theory – quite a lot of theatre history, theories connected with theatre and performance practice at the present time. But there were also opportunities to devise our own performances, do some video editing and things like that. So it was a very broad spectrum that the degree covered. The most interesting part of the course to me was the variety. In my third year there was an extended period of devising my own show with a student colleague. This was a mixture of live performance and video. So we projected video images on screens and performed in front of them.

I found it particularly interesting working with video. And there was the opportunity to do a whole module in learning about video editing and the techniques involved in filming.

While I was at university I worked in the box office at the Warwick Arts Centre – a big multipurpose arts venue showing opera, film and drama and so on. I think it's the second largest arts venue in the country, second only to the Barbican.

When I graduated I think I realised that in order for me to work in an arts venue, which I wanted to do, I would have to draw on the skills that I'd got working at the arts centre and at the Merlin in Frome. I started looking around at administration and marketing jobs advertised in the national press. And in the October after graduating in June I got a job here at the Marlowe Theatre. That was quite quick I guess. I think the job I have now is the first one I applied for. But I was actually the second choice, so it took me a while to get into it.

I have been with the Marlowe for ten months now. The job was advertised as a training position, designed to last a year and to give an insight into arts marketing. There are two of us working at the theatre in the same position. The intention is that it leads on to managing a marketing department, or moving on somewhere else in arts administration. But I'm still trying to make up my mind as to which direction I want to go afterwards.

Experience definitely does pay in this area. Having done this should put me in a good position when looking for other jobs.

The most useful skill I learned when at university was how to operate in a busy office environment. I also developed skills in designing and printing publicity material for the theatre, and computer software.

Advising someone considering studying an arts or humanities subject, I would say that I didn't do my degree because I wanted there to be a particular job at the end of it. I did it because I was interested in the subject that I studied. So I would say 'do the same'. I had a great time at university. Don't worry too much about what you are going to do at the end of it. Just go up and enjoy the experience.'

Sales

Selling is about persuading people to buy your products. Salespeople call on potential and existing customers. They identify customer needs through discussion and then show how the company's product can satisfy that customer's needs better than those of its competitors. The sales department often becomes the customer's main point of contact with the company: processing fresh orders, dealing with queries, and resolving any problems that customers may have through incorrect or late deliveries, product faults or other mistakes. So far as the customer is concerned, the salesperson is the company. Salespeople may work closely with marketing staff, following up leads for new business or passing on customer feedback about the products. You will find more information about different forms of selling jobs in Chapter twenty.

Production

Products are made in many ways. These include computer-controlled production lines for making items such as cars, CDs and chocolates. There are continuous process plants like oil and chemical refineries. There are assembly lines in which people build up parts into finished products such as clocks and computers, assemble mass-produced garments, or sort fruit and vegetables for freezing or canning. Other products may be 'one-offs' and made to order – buildings, television films, wedding cakes and cruise liners.

Buying

All organisations need to buy goods and materials to go about their business. Manufacturers buy raw materials and components to make their products. This is not just a matter of negotiating a good price, but also of securing consistent quality and guaranteed delivery times. Reliability of supply is essential – no employer wants machines or people idle when there are orders waiting to be filled. Some materials can be in scarce supply, and buyers may have to seek out suppliers worldwide.

Retailers buy goods for resale, either direct from manufacturers (who may be anywhere in the world) or from wholesalers. You will be concerned with establishing customer buying trends and finding the products to satisfy them. There will be a lot of forward planning: for example, retail perfumery buyers look for Christmas goods in the spring. In service industries, buyers are responsible for acquiring all those supplies necessary for their business to operate – for instance, in hotels they might buy everything from buildings to bedding, security to soap and food to furniture.

Logistics

This used to be called warehousing and transport. After goods are made or purchased, they are traditionally stored until needed. Then, when required, they are distributed in such a way that they reach the customer on time and in perfect condition. Customers may be anywhere in the world. Reliability is essential. Controlling costs by careful route planning and by using the right sized vehicles for each delivery is also vital. More recently, some businesses have adopted 'just-in-time' working – so that goods and components are delivered to a production line only a few hours before they are assembled into the finished product or delivered to a supermarket and put on display. For instance, this is common in motor manufacturing. So suppliers' lorries from all round the country deliver carefully scheduled supplies of body panels, windscreens, wheels and all the other components needed to keep the production line running. One late delivery of a single component can bring production to a halt.

Accounting and finance

Every business must keep full details of all its financial transactions and have them audited each year. These include invoices sent to customers and received from suppliers, payments received and sent out, wages, rents, rates, taxes (such as VAT), fees for professional services and so on.

To control the money going in and out of a business, and to make sure more isn't spent than comes in, each department works to a budget. Departmental managers need to know, monthly or even more often, how they are doing against their budgets through a system of 'management accounting'. Many businesses finance growth by borrowing money to build new premises, buy more or better equipment, hire more staff, and so on. Those that import or export goods often need to buy and sell foreign currency. There are many openings for graduates in the financial management of business – these are discussed in more detail in Chapter eighteen.

Computing or management services

Virtually all organisations use computers for their financial records, market statistics, sales data, production planning, stock control, customer information, personnel records and so on. The work covers analysing the information needs of each department, and designing and running integrated management systems. For this reason, what used to be called computing is now often called management services. This calls for creativity as much as technical knowledge.

Human resource (HR) or personnel management

A business must recruit, train and develop staff for every function. It must also care for everyone's health, safety and welfare, make sure that people are paid fairly, deal with equal opportunities, negotiate with trades unions, possibly provide canteens and other facilities, and much more. Many HR people, particularly in large organisations, specialise in such areas as recruitment or training. Although each of these functions is a specialist activity, and will have specialist managers, they are all interdependent and form part of an organic whole. The managers of each area must collaborate as one team to run the business successfully.

'It is this interdependence of functions which determines the way in which managers work. Everyone has to start in one function, but none of us, however specialist our role, can work in isolation. We are part of a multidisciplinary team working towards shared objectives and we must be constantly aware of how our own function interacts with those of our colleagues and with the organisation as a whole. We must work together, not just with our peers, but with colleagues at all levels.'

Graduate recruitment brochure

What do managers do?

In traditionally organised companies, managers head a department, or section of a department, and lead a team of people. This is usually known as 'line management'.

Managers are assessed on the performance of their team. Line managers report to senior managers who plan, coordinate and supervise the activities of all the specialist departments so that they work together as a single organisation. This level is known as 'general management'.

However, you may remember from Chapter three that many employers now have fewer layers of management than in the past and so have to organise their work in new ways. More work is carried out by project teams, which are put together on the basis of the skills and knowledge needed and stay together only for the duration of a specific job. In this type of work you move from one project to another. On some you may lead the team because you have the relevant skills or experience, on others you will be managed by someone else. For you, following a management career, the biggest difference is that in a project management structure, you may not have responsibility for a permanent team of your own staff.

Whichever system of working is in place, most managers are concerned mainly with operational management. This involves implementing policy decisions and organising resources so that the activities of the business run smoothly and profitably. (Setting strategy and making policy decisions tend to be the responsibility of more senior managers who have the necessary overview of the organisation.)

It is useful to look in more detail at the six main functions of managers described earlier under 'What is management?'. As an operational manager, you will typically:

- plan the work of the department or section
- attend planning and other meetings
- prepare budgets and get them agreed by senior management

- set team and individual targets

- ensure you have the resources that your department needs

- monitor team and individual performance, making sure that targets are met

- monitor the quality of the work done by members of your staff

- keep records and monitor them against targets and budgets

- report to senior management

- train, develop, supervise and motivate your staff

- keep your staff informed about what's going on within the organisation

- constantly seek better ways of doing things

- solve problems when they arise

- liaise with managers in other departments

- liaise with suppliers and customers.

Managers often find it difficult to plan much of their working day, because problems can arise at any moment and must often be dealt with at once.

'Managers are engaged in a vast range of activities, many of which are also invisible – like thinking! These activities are very fragmented, and many tasks may only take a matter of minutes. The pattern of activity varies from job to job, and job holders may also have considerable choice in how they choose to define and carry out their tasks.'

**'Defining Managerial Skills',
Institute for Employment Studies**

Are managers the same as executives?

Although the words manager and executive are often used to mean the same thing, they are different. A manager is someone who leads a team of people. An executive is an expert who makes decisions that can affect the whole organisation's future, and who must take responsibility for those decisions. Executives are supposed to have the specialist knowledge that should make them better qualified than anyone else to make the right decision.

Many managers are executives, but not all. Supervisors in shops or on a factory floor are managers because they manage the work of others, but they are not executives with the expertise to make policy decisions. On the other hand, many non-managers are executives because of their expertise.

Most modern organisations need both managers and individual experts. An increasing proportion of graduate jobs are in 'expert' roles. But most employers still organise work in fairly traditional ways. Unless you're a science or technology graduate, you're unlikely to find yourself in an 'executive' role without firstly gaining experience in line management.

Although 'manager' and 'executive' are often used in misleading ways, don't worry about it. Most organisations use the language of management, including job titles, in different ways. Once you join an employer, you'll soon get used to your organisation's internal language.

"When I use a word,' Humpty Dumpty said, in rather a scornful tone, 'it means just what I choose it to mean – neither more nor less'.'

Lewis Carroll, *Alice Through the Looking Glass*

Management consultancy

Management consultants advise organisations how to manage their affairs more effectively. Often, they are brought in to solve a specific problem or to conduct feasibility studies. They are more executives than managers. Newly-qualified graduates are sometimes recruited into management consultancy and then trained to do the job. The employers most likely to do this are the larger chartered accountancy firms. This does not mean that you have to become a chartered accountant, but you do need an exceptional level of analytical and problem-solving skills. It may be helpful to read the chartered accountancy section of the next chapter.

What qualities do you need?

If you like getting your head down to concentrate on one thing at a time without interruption, then management probably isn't for you. You probably won't enjoy it either if you prefer to do things yourself rather than depend on others to do them. You need to be flexible, a good team worker and able to motivate those around you to share your vision. Effective managers earn the willing respect and cooperation of their team. They do not use their rank to 'boss people about'.

You need to be reasonably self-confident, have good social skills and be able to communicate clearly and persuasively, orally and in writing. (These qualities and skills are especially important in management consultancy.) You must be able to earn the respect of others, including those over whom you've no direct authority. You'll also have to collaborate with managers at all levels throughout the organisation. In dealing with others, you must be able to argue your point of view persuasively and persistently, and yet be willing to listen and learn, and make compromises when appropriate.

In your early days you may be responsible for leading people who have many more years of specialist experience than you. You need to listen to your staff and show that you are willing to learn from them. You must know when to admit your own lack of expertise and ask for help. This is a sign of strength, not weakness.

The best managers employ high-calibre people and train and develop them so that they become as good or better than themselves at the job. Only weak managers want low-calibre subservient staff or 'yes men'. This, too, takes self-confidence, knowing you've good people ready to step into your shoes. However, remember that managers are usually judged on the calibre of the people they develop – and they can't easily be promoted themselves unless someone is ready to be promoted in their place.

'Here lies a man
Who knew how to enlist
In his service
Better men than himself.'

**Epitaph of Andrew Carnegie, Scottish-American
businessman and philanthropist**

All managers need the key skills described in Chapter four. You may find it helpful to remind yourself of these. Some employers in their recruitment brochures and advertisements also ask that applicants for their vacancies are ambitious. It's worth looking at this in a bit more detail.

What do employers mean by ambition?

Ambition to some people is the competitive spirit that drives a person to try and get to the top. To others it's the pursuit of excellence. Many people, including some employers, think ambition is the same as competitiveness. Because businesses must compete with one another in the marketplace to survive and prosper, it is assumed that competition between individuals within a firm is also good.

But as we've already seen, the functions of an organisation interact with one another. Similarly, the work of each person within a function interacts with that of colleagues. Unless their aims and work pace are mutually compatible, the organisation can't function properly. An organisation, like a sports team, is a group of individuals each with a specific role and responsibilities. Can you imagine how well a sports team would do if all the players competed against one another as well as against their opponents?

This doesn't mean that good team players must lose their individuality and become faceless cogs in a machine. You can still show individual brilliance and earn personal recognition. In most companies, therefore, ambition is seen as the desire to achieve excellence within a function and the willingness to accept increasing levels of responsibility up to your full potential – but not beyond it. In these organisations, management authority comes from recognised expertise and the ability to collaborate with others, not from one's rank in the hierarchy.

Entry qualifications

There are two usual entry routes into a management career – the traditional management training scheme, usually run only by large organisations, and direct entry. The management training scheme is designed for the few 'high-flyers' capable of progressing through line management to general management relatively quickly. Most graduates are now recruited by direct entry, in which you join a specific function and are trained on the job.

Do be wary of the wording in recruitment brochures: some direct entry schemes are also called traineeships, so make sure you know exactly what it is that you are applying for. Management traineeships are usually aimed only at those with the potential to reach the top of general management.

For either route, any degree subject is normally acceptable – although rigorous disciplines are preferred. Although management trainee vacancies fell in recent years, the number is now increasing again. But competition for places remains intense. Moreover, the Association of Graduate Recruiters (AGR) reported that during the 2004-2005 recruitment season a total of 17% of its members faced difficulties filling their graduate vacancies. The main reason given was a lack of applicants with suitable skills – namely leadership, communication and business skills.

You will usually need at least a good second-class honours first degree. A lower level may be acceptable for direct entry. A postgraduate qualification, unless it's in a relevant business subject, is unlikely to give you any further advantage for either type of entry.

The most critical qualification is what employers usually call 'personal qualities'. This generally means the key skills described in Chapter four. You should develop these as far as you can before you graduate. Work experience (from Saturday jobs, holiday work, helping in a family business, work placements linked to your studies, and so on) is especially valued. If you are attracted to working in business, it is worth remembering that a language could also be valuable – for instance, over 60% of British companies conduct business with foreigners whose first language is not English.

'Français parle ici.'

Sign in an English shop window

A survey of 2000 companies by the Institute for Employment Studies found that 'Language needs were highly concentrated in a few language areas: predominantly French and German speaking countries, followed by Spanish and Italian; these were the countries where business was most often conducted and where business could least often be adequately conducted in English.' There is also a significant need for people with Japanese, Arabic, Dutch and the languages of Eastern Europe. Mandarin Chinese is also likely to become one of the most important languages of all because China, with a population five times greater than the United States, is fast emerging as a major world economy.

Training and career development

Your initial training and career development will differ according to whether you are on a 'high-flyer' management training scheme or direct entry. However, in the long term both groups have similar opportunities to reach the top.

Traditional management training

This type of scheme usually lasts 18-24 months and typically combines formal business education, skills training and project work. You're likely to spend time in a number of functions. This will help you to understand how the business works as a whole, and to find out which specialist area is best suited to your interests and aptitudes.

Once you move into a specialist area you may, depending on your function, be expected to combine your internal management training with study for membership of an appropriate professional institution. This is often equivalent to studying for another degree. Typical qualifications for which you might study are those of The Chartered Institute of Marketing, The Chartered Institute of Management Accounting or The Chartered Institute of Personnel and Development. You'll usually get day release and possibly some study leave before your examinations, and your employer will pay your fees and other expenses – but most of your study will be in your free time.

Although you'll have undertaken project work and spent time helping managers in various departments, you won't take up a management post of your own until your formal training period is over. Even then, you'll continue with any professional studies you may have started.

Your career development will then be up to you. As a potential 'high-flyer' you can expect regular moves upwards into jobs of increasing responsibility, and laterally through different functions.

Direct entry

If you are a direct entrant you will have a few days of 'induction training' to learn about the organisation, the goods or services it provides, its systems and so on. You will then start your job. Initially, you will work under close supervision – being trained on the job. You are likely to go on courses from time to time. Some will cover generic management skills – such as making presentations, writing reports, preparing budgets and understanding balance sheets. Others may deal with technical aspects of your job function.

Depending on your function, you may be able to study for a relevant professional qualification. However, you may have to take the initiative yourself. If you do, your employer is likely to give you a lot of support.

It's well worth getting a professional qualification if you can. It will not only enhance your prospects with your existing employer, but also give you a valuable qualification to help you get a new job if you decide to move.

Career progression

For direct entrants, career progression is usually within the specialist function in which you start, at least for several years. But by the time you reach your early 30s, you should also get opportunities to broaden your experience in other functions.

Up to this point, 'high-flyers' on a management training scheme should have gained wider experience and made faster progress. On the other hand, their employer will have had very high expectations of them. Many will have peaked early and direct entrants now have the chance to overtake them. From this point onwards, it won't matter whether you started on a management training scheme or through direct entry.

As you become more senior you become increasingly concerned with coordinating the activities of different functions, and so move into general management. To prepare you for this you are likely to undertake a further programme of management education. Your employer could even send you to business school, most probably on a two-year part-time Masters degree in Business Administration (MBA) course, although a few may be sent on a one-year full-time course, sometimes overseas.

Finding vacancies

During your second year, visit your university careers service (sometimes called an appointments service) and discuss your career interests with a careers adviser. At the beginning of your final academic year you should collect a free copy of each of the two major graduate careers directories, *Graduate Employment and Training* (GET) and *Prospects Directory*. Details of these are in Chapter twenty-two.

These directories contain employer entries that describe what they do, the careers on offer, the qualities needed, training schemes, and the approximate number of vacancies. From these you can produce a shortlist of employers that interest you most. Although some entries are duplicated in both directories, each contains some information not in the other, so it is worth looking at both. It is also worth looking at the websites of both publishers: www.get.hobsons.com and www.prospects.csu.ac.uk

The careers service should have copies of brochures provided by most, if not all, of your short-listed employers. These will give you much more detailed information about the organisation and what it has to offer. They will also tell you how to apply and will either include an application form or tell you how to get one.

You should also look at the websites of those employers that interest you. They have the most up-to-date information on the organisation (and organisations change rapidly nowadays) and also on their vacancies. You should also be aware that more than half of AGR members (56%) now only accept online applications.

Some employers make on-campus presentations to students in the autumn term. These also offer the opportunity to talk to members of their staff to get a feel for the organisation. Your careers service will also keep a file on each major employer that you can consult. This usually contains a copy of the graduate brochure, the annual report, current data on vacancies and salaries, newspaper and magazine articles and news cuttings, and so on.

Half of applications for management traineeships have a cut-off date in December or January – so apply early. Don't leave your job search until after you graduate. Early applicants are perceived to be brighter, more energetic and more motivated than later applicants.

Employers in the financial sector visit universities to conduct first interviews in the autumn term. Other employers do so in the spring term. These visits are known as the 'milkround' because employers are seeking 'the cream' of the graduates. Although the milkround is used less than in the past, it is still an important way of recruiting high-flyers for management traineeships.

If you don't find anything suitable through the milkround, look for graduate recruitment advertisements in the 'quality' national newspapers, in *Prospects Finalist* (for those yet to graduate) and *Prospects Today* (for immediate vacancies) and on the internet. Both Prospects publications are available free from your careers service and are also on the Prospects website: www.prospects.ac.uk

If by your final term you have found nothing, visit one of the summer fairs. These are organised by universities and are attended by employers who have unfilled vacancies. However, do not rely on fairs for your main job search – only a minority of graduate vacancies are filled in this way.

Vacancies in Europe

With our membership of the European Union, you can seek work in other member states. But you need to be reasonably fluent in at least one other European language and show some cultural sensitivity. However, it is fairly difficult to find suitable posts in other European countries and could remain so for some time. Recruitment systems and employment cultures vary a lot across the Union and you will not find the same career structures open to you everywhere. This should change in time, and the European Commission is organising systems, such as EURES (http://europa.eu.int/eures). This is a Europe-wide database containing information on vacancies, living conditions and employment terms.

Meanwhile, there are two main options you could consider if you want a European focus to your management career. Firstly, there are many UK-based organisations – such as Barclays (operating in more than 60 countries) and Mars (in 65 countries) – that provide opportunities to work in mainland Europe as well as the UK. Secondly, you could consider a career in European public service, for example working for one of the institutions of the European Union. There is more about this in Chapter fifteen.

If you are interested in these options, watch out for any opportunities to visit international recruitment fairs. You will also find details of recruitment directories for some other European countries in Chapter twenty-two.

Chapter eighteen
Careers in financial services

Most people think that anything to do with finance involves lots of maths, but this is a fallacy. For most finance careers you only need fairly good basic arithmetic (say at GCSE level) and a reasonably analytical mind so you can interpret simple statistical data. Only a few specialist areas, such as actuarial work, need a high level of mathematical skill. In most financial services it is far more important that you are good with people and that you have good communication skills.

The main functions, which will be looked at in turn, are accountancy, banking and building society work, insurance, stockbroking and actuarial work.

Accountancy

Accountancy has an ill-deserved reputation for being boring. And it is true that the learning you've got to do before you become professionally qualified can be tedious. But an independent research study of accountants in early and mid-career by the Institute for Employment Studies found unusually high levels of job satisfaction. For instance, more than eight in ten said that they find enjoyment in the job, three-quarters said that they are doing interesting and challenging work, and a similar number said that they have no regrets about choosing accountancy as a career.

Accountants are concerned with managing money. They prepare and analyse accounts for businesses and provide expert financial advice. The image of desk-bound number crunchers is false: accountants have to understand the whole business of the organisations they serve. Consequently, they get out and about quite a lot. A lot of their time is spent talking to people. Moreover, the training for an accountancy qualification is excellent preparation for a general management career in almost any area of the economy. Accountancy training can also be good preparation for someone who wants to start and run their own business (see Chapter twenty) because it can develop both business awareness and knowledge of financial management.

Every organisation is required by law to keep 'books' or 'accounts'. These are records of all items of income or expenditure. These records, which increasingly are computerised, form the basis of the annual accounts. All but the very smallest limited companies must, by law, have these accounts 'audited', i.e. checked that they are a 'true and fair view' of the company's affairs. Only a 'chartered' or 'certified' accountant from outside the organisation can carry out an audit.

There are three main areas in which accountants work:

- industry and commerce
- public practice (confusingly also called private practice)
- public service.

The emphasis on financial accounting, management accounting and auditing in your work will vary according to which field you join. There is specialist training for each.

Financial accountants

These accountants are usually company employees who keep and analyse records of company income and expenditure, produce annual accounts for shareholders and HM Revenue and Customs, interpret financial information and borrow money for the business . They also ensure that salaries and bills are paid, and that customers are invoiced and pay their bills on time.

Management accountants

These too are usually company employees. If you become a management accountant you may examine policies and long-term plans, look at the costs and benefits of different business strategies, and present your findings to top management. They also help to prepare budgets and monitor the performance of departments against their budgets. Their work involves talking to colleagues throughout the business and providing them with advice. In effect, they are internal consultants. They often move into the consultancy sections of public practice firms or into management consultancy firms.

Public practice accountants

These accountants work in firms of partners. The core of their work consists of auditing company accounts and giving technical advice on taxation. They may also produce annual accounts on behalf of self-employed individuals and small businesses. Many larger public practice firms, which also provide insolvency and consultancy services, also have a network of regional offices, while others work from a central location – often London. There are also many local firms.

Auditing

This work is carried out in clients' offices and may involve a lot of travel and time away from home. Apart from checking financial records, both manual and computerised, an audit usually involves interviewing staff at all levels to find out about various aspects of the figures. Audits can last from a day or two to several months, depending on the size of the company. Although auditing used to be considered boring, computers and new systems have removed a lot of the drudgery of routine checking – what used to be called 'tick and bash'. And if you look beyond the figures and see what lies behind them, auditing is a very good way of studying a variety of businesses from the inside and learning how they work.

Taxation and insolvency

Taxation work involves giving advice and negotiating tax assessments with the HM Revenue and Customs on behalf of various clients. Insolvency work involves dealing with the financial affairs of businesses that face bankruptcy or have already been declared bankrupt. This may include trying to save the business, selling the business as a going concern or, failing all else, selling off the assets so that creditors (the people the business owes money to) can be paid.

Consultancy

This work can involve advising organisations on any aspect of their business that will enable them to improve their efficiency and profitability.

Public service accountants

These work for central and local government, the National Health Service and publicly owned utilities. They also work in the five bodies that audit public service accounts:

- The National Audit Office (central government and other public sector bodies)

- The Audit Commission (local government and NHS in England)

- Audit Scotland (all public sector in Scotland)

- The Northern Ireland Audit Office (all public sector in Northern Ireland)

- Audit Wales (all public sector in Wales).

Public service accountants, like those in industry and commerce, are concerned with all aspects of financial management, but particularly with the efficient use of taxpayers' money and ensuring that the public gets value for money. Value for money (VFM) studies are an important part of their work. Like those in industry and commerce, many public sector accountants eventually move into top-level general management.

Entry qualifications

The accountancy bodies accept any degree subject. In addition, they normally expect you to have GCSE grades A*-C in mathematics and English (or their equivalents). You'll need curiosity, an analytical mind and a logical and methodical approach to your work. You should also be comfortable working with computers. A lot of the work involves asking questions, giving advice and explaining financial matters to non-specialists, so you'll need to get on with people at all levels and be able to express yourself clearly both orally and in writing.

Training

Accountants usually qualify with one of six accountancy bodies. These are:

- Institute of Chartered Accountants in England and Wales (ICAEW)

- Institute of Chartered Accountants of Scotland (ICAS)

- Institute of Chartered Accountants in Ireland (ICAI)

- Association of Chartered Certified Accountants (ACCA)

- Chartered Institute of Management Accountants (CIMA)

- Chartered Institute of Public Finance and Accountancy (CIPFA).

To enter public practice you must qualify for one of the first four bodies, because only chartered and certified accountants may audit company accounts. Chartered and certified accountants also work in industry, commerce and the public sector and so have the widest choice of career options.

If you are interested in the profitable and efficient running of businesses, CIMA may be more appropriate. Members can also work in the public sector.

Members of CIPFA work almost entirely in central and local government, the NHS and public utilities, and their qualification is geared to this. But, it's worth noting that some public sector employers, including the National Audit Office and some regional health authorities, now prefer the ICAEW.

Training for professional membership of any of the institutes normally involves three years of relevant work experience during which you also study for professional examinations. You shouldn't underestimate the difficulty of these studies. They are equivalent to taking another degree, usually while doing a full-time job.

There are some differences in the approach of the individual institutions. To become a chartered accountant you enter a three- to five-year training contract either with a firm of chartered accountants (the traditional route) or with an industrial or commercial company or government department approved by the Institute. In England and Wales you usually work almost full time (sometimes doing overtime) and do most of your theoretical studies in your own time. In Scotland, and in some of the largest English practices, you are given periods of time off (called 'block release') to attend one of the Institute's own education centres.

Most of those studying for the CIPFA qualification are employed in the public sector, although you don't have to be. Training with the ACCA CIMA and CIPFA is more flexible. You don't enter a training contract and are free to change employers and type of work while under training. With the ACCA you can choose to study for your exams full time, either before or after getting your three years of 'relevant accountancy experience' that you also need in order to qualify. Most students studying for the CIPFA qualification do so while working in the public sector – although you can qualify while working in professional accountancy firms, industry or commerce.

Career development

Once qualified, you can progress in many ways. CIPFA members, once confined to public sector organisations, can now choose to enter top management in industry. Chartered and certified accountants can become partners in public practice or, like CIMA members, advance to the highest management levels in industry and commerce.

Finding training vacancies

Each institute publishes details of some of the available training vacancies on its website. Details of many others can be found in your regional and national press and in the major careers directories (*GET* and *Prospects Directory*). Your careers service should have details of others and also be able to let you have a copy of the graduate recruitment brochures of the institutions that interest you.

Institute of Chartered Accountants in England and Wales – Student Recruitment and Promotion, Gloucester House, 399 Silbury Boulevard, Central Milton Keynes MK9 2HL. Tel: 01908 248040. www.icaew.co.uk

Institute of Chartered Accountants of Scotland – CA House, 21 Haymarket Yards, Edinburgh EH12 5BH. Tel: 0131 347 0100. www.icas.org.uk

Institute of Chartered Accountants in Ireland – 11 Donegal Square South, Belfast BT1 5JE. Tel: 028 9032 1600. www.icai.ie – or, CA House, 83 Pembroke Road, Dublin 4, Eire. Tel: 353 1 637 7200. www.icai.ie

Association of Chartered Certified Accountants – 29 Lincoln's Inn Fields, London WC2A 3EE. Tel: 020 7059 5700. www.accaglobal.com

Chartered Institute of Management Accountants – 26 Chapter Street, London SW1P 4NP. Tel: 020 7663 5441. www.cimaglobal.com

Chartered Institute of Public Finance and Accountancy – 3 Robert Street, London WC2N 6RL. Tel: 020 7543 5600. www.cipfa.org.uk

Banks and building societies

In the past twenty years there has been a continuing revolution in the financial sector, including retail banking and building societies. If you are to consider a career in this area, it is helpful to understand a little of what has happened. Clearing or retail banks, which are owned by shareholders, handled most of the country's retail or personal banking. They took deposits and made loans, cleared cheques, transferred funds and sold a range of 'financial products' to individuals and organisations. In the past the clearing banks all provided similar services at similar costs. Competition was minimal.

On the other hand, building societies had two main functions. They encouraged people to save by paying them interest on money deposited with the society. They also encouraged home ownership by providing mortgages from the money deposited with them. Building societies were not owned by shareholders but by their members – the people who deposited money with them or who took out mortgages from them. For this reason they were called 'mutual societies'.

Then, the UK branches of American-based banks started to sell their services aggressively and other institutions introduced new financial services. Shocked out of their inertia, British banks started to market their services and to introduce new ones – such as credit cards, personal loans, cash machines, mortgages and investment advice.

They also began to streamline their administrative and communication systems using the latest information and communication technology (ICT).

In 1986 came 'the Big Bang', the day the UK financial market was deregulated. Until then, people buying or selling shares in companies had to use stockbrokers – agents who all charged the same rate of commission. Acting on clients' instructions, stockbrokers bought from or sold to 'jobbers' (now called 'market makers'). Brokers, jobbers and bankers were kept separate and distinct. But 'the Big Bang' changed all that.

Banks and other institutions were allowed to join the Stock Exchange (properly called the London Stock Exchange). Banks bought up stockbroking and jobbing firms, other firms merged. Today, we have banking groups offering a wide range of services, so the distinctions between different types of financial institution have blurred or vanished.

All this prompted the building societies to widen their range of services and start to compete more directly with the banks. This costs money. Because it is easier for a public company like a bank to borrow money in the City than it is for a mutual society, many building societies gave up their mutual status and converted to banks.

Banks may be grouped into four broad types. These are:

- clearing banks and building societies
- investment banks
- the Bank of England
- international banks.

Clearing banks and building societies

These have become highly commercial. Banks offer the full range of financial services, while buildings societies still concentrate on a wide variety of savings accounts, providing mortgages to home buyers, selling insurance and, in some cases, running chains of estate agencies. As I've already noted, the distinctions between the two are increasingly blurred. Moreover, although some building societies still survive, they have become much fewer in number and it is possible that more will 'demutualise' and convert to banks.

Both continue to make a massive investment in ICT. They have also shed large numbers of junior staff as ICT has taken over a lot of the routine clerical work. However, they do invest heavily in developing graduates as their future technical specialists and managers.

Branch management

Managers in clearing banks and building societies are responsible for running branches profitably. They lead a team that opens and monitors bank accounts for individuals and businesses, handles enquiries, assesses credit risks and provides loans, sells insurance, arranges mortgages and offers financial advice. Branches are organised into districts. In a district where branches are fairly small, a manager may be responsible for two or more branches. Branch managers can authorise loans only up to a fixed limit. Requests for loans above this limit are analysed at district or head office level.

Managers in banks spend a lot of time visiting businesses – discussing their business plans, loans, insurance and other needs. Managers in building societies spend more of their time visiting accountants, solicitors, estate agents, builders, surveyors and so on. They also spend time with customers who come to them for pensions and investment advice. Sometimes they also have to interview customers who have difficulty paying their mortgages.

Investment banking

Corporate or merchant bankers provide services similar to the retail banks but to customers who range from small businesses to multinational corporations and overseas governments. The scale and complexity of the work is much greater. As well as taking deposits, making loans and transferring funds, the work of merchant bankers includes financing international trade, advising on mergers and takeovers, and raising capital. They buy and sell foreign currency (known as foreign exchange) and manage pension funds and investment trusts. They help companies acquire assets, such as a fleet of new lorries, by buying them and leasing them to the customer. They are also involved in floating companies on the stock market and buying and selling shares.

There is an overlap between retail and corporate banking – with retail banks serving some business needs. And, although there are independent investment banks, many are now subsidiaries of clearing banks. This means that graduates in most banks can transfer between the two areas.

The Bank of England

This bank is at the centre of economic and financial policy making in the UK. It acts as banker to the Government and to the other banks.

Much of its work involves the collection, analysis and interpretation of economic and financial data relating both to the British economy and to economic conditions abroad.

International banks

Naturally, as trade becomes more international, so do banking services. Because London is a world-class financial centre, banks from all over the world have London branches. Similarly, a number of UK banks also have branches overseas – Barclays operates in more than 60 countries. These offices serve individuals as well as companies involved in international trade, though these banks primarily provide corporate banking services.

Many overseas banks are attracted to London because the market is relatively unregulated and the time zone gives same-day access to the Far East and Far West stock markets. English is normally the working language, and many overseas banks recruit British graduates.

Even so, because much of the work involves serving overseas clients, a knowledge of another language is valuable. As well as the direct banking careers, there are openings in specialist roles such as audit, accountancy, actuarial work, and ICT (usually called management services – see Chapter twenty).

Entry qualifications

Banks and building societies accept any degree (often a 2.1 or better), although some corporate banks prefer a business-related subject. The Bank of England will consider any degree subject, but prefers graduates who have an economics or related degree; language skills (especially European, Japanese, Russian and increasingly Mandarin) are also helpful. Because most banks and building societies have large branch networks, you are normally required to be mobile and able to lead a team. Above all, because you're offering services to people at all levels up to the most senior, you'll need mature social skills and must communicate clearly and persuasively.

Training and development

You'll join a graduate training programme that will combine work experience in a variety of functions with a programme of study. These studies lead to professional membership of the Chartered Institute of Bankers (CIB). The CIB is the parent body of The Institute of Financial Services (IFS), which provides a range of banking and other qualifications appropriate to the wider financial services industry. These qualifications have the advantage of being portable between various sectors of the financial services industry.

Graduates, and those aspiring to a management position, will normally study part time for a BSc (Hons) in financial services and Associateship of the CIB. This is a highly respected qualification. Progress depends on your performance. You may move up in management roles of increasing seniority or become a specialist in a particular area of banking such as international banking, investment management for institutional clients, and treasury (buying and selling foreign currency).

Finding vacancies

Many banks and building societies advertise in the annual directories (*Graduate Employment and Training (GET)* and *Prospects Directory*), which you can get free from your graduate careers service. Most will also tell your careers service of their requirements for the following year. Some also advertise in national 'quality' newspapers. Most also produce graduate recruitment brochures available from your university careers service. You can also find more information on the web.

Further information

Chartered Institute of Bankers – IFS House, 4-9 Burgate Lane, Canterbury, Kent CT1 2XJ. Tel: 01227 762600. www.ifslearning.com

Chartered Institute of Bankers in Scotland – Drumsheugh House, 38b Drumsheugh Gardens, Edinburgh EH3 7SW. Tel: 0131 473 777. www.ciobs.org.uk

Institute of Financial Services – IFS House, 4-9 Burgate Lane, Canterbury, Kent CT1 2XJ. Tel: 01227 762600. www.ifslearning.com

Insurance

Insurance is a way of protecting people from losses arising from sickness, theft, fire, accident and other misfortunes. Insurance is based on the laws of probability: that is, the likelihood of certain events occurring or happening to people. The principle behind it is that many people regularly pay into a common fund but only a few people will need to claim compensation for a mishap.

Insurance cover can be provided for practically anything: from a second-hand car to a jumbo jet or from a paint factory to a painting by Leonardo da Vinci. At a more personal level, you can insure against a cancelled holiday, having twins, losing a limb, or having your home burgled.

Insurance in Britain is provided by more than 450 insurance companies and by Lloyd's of London. Lloyd's is not a company but an insurance 'market' where the risks are carried by syndicates of individuals. Each syndicate has an underwriter who accepts business on behalf of syndicate members. There are also insurance brokers, independent specialists who advise on and negotiate insurance policies on behalf of their clients. Most brokers specialise in a particular area such as motors, marine or aviation.

A career in insurance

The four areas of insurance work, which you, as an arts or humanities graduate, might consider are:

- underwriting

- insurance surveying

- claims assessment

- selling.

Insurance is offered against the risk of specific incidents taking place. You don't insure a person, event or object – you insure against something happening to that person, event or object.

The work of underwriters

Underwriters, both in the insurance companies and those in Lloyd's, are responsible for calculating the risks, deciding whether they are insurable and, if so, on what terms. Some risks are simple to assess and are based on standard guidelines. Others, such as the Channel Tunnel or a space satellite are more complex. As an underwriter you may have to calculate the risk of an aircraft crashing, a factory burning down, an oil rig being destroyed by a hurricane, a film star becoming ill during filming or many other types of mishap. Insurance is very competitive – so if an underwriter sets the premium too high the company may lose business to its competitors. If premiums are set too low, claims may exceed premiums. This happened at Lloyd's a few years ago, and syndicate members lost huge sums of money.

The work of surveyors

In the case of commercial properties, underwriters may seek the advice of surveyors who will report on any aspects that might affect the underwriter's assessment, such as the use of dangerous materials, fire risks and security. Surveyors also advise clients on how to reduce their risks (and so their premiums) through improved security, safer storage of flammable materials and so on. Insurance surveyors are often drawn from existing staff and given appropriate training. They are not necessarily chartered surveyors.

The work of claims staff

When claims are made, claims staff assess the loss and decide the amount to be paid. Some claim assessments are quite simple; others may require expert knowledge of medicine, the law, or some aspect of science or technology. For large, complex or disputed claims, the insurer may bring in a loss adjuster to examine the claim and help to reach a settlement. The insured party may also employ their own independent loss adjuster to negotiate the claim on their behalf.

The work of insurance agents

The other main area of work in insurance is selling to the general public and to insurance brokers and agents. (You can find more on selling in Chapter seven.) You should also look at the information on actuarial work at the end of this chapter.

Entry qualifications

Any degree subject is acceptable. You also need to be numerate, to have an analytical mind and to be able to combine assertiveness with tact (you may have to deal sensitively with people who have suffered various calamities). You must be a persuasive communicator, both orally and in writing.

Training and career development

You are likely to join a graduate training programme that will combine on-the-job work experience, in a variety of functions, with part-time study.

Although the industry employs graduates in a number of specialisations, the central educational and professional body for most people is the Chartered Insurance Institute (CII). The Institute has around 90,000 members and offers its own examinations and qualifications. As a graduate, you will be eligible to study for the exams leading to Associate membership – which is a recognised professional qualification. Following a programme of Continuing Professional Development (CPD) for at least another three years will qualify you for Fellowship.

Finding vacancies

Check the information in the annual careers directories (*Graduate Employment and Training (GET)* and *Prospects Directory*) obtainable free from your graduate careers service, and also consult the web. Large insurance companies are also likely to send details of their vacancies for the following year direct to your careers service. Others advertise their vacancies in national 'quality' newspapers.

Further information

You can get more information on career prospects in insurance, and on the professional examinations of the CII from:

The Chartered Insurance Institute – Careers Information Officer, 20 Aldermanbury, London EC2V 7HY. Tel: 020 74174415/6. www.cii.co.uk

Lloyds – One Lime Street, London EC3M 7HA. Tel: 0207 327 1000. www.lloyds.com

Stockbroking

The London Stock Exchange is a marketplace where industry, commerce and the Government can raise money by selling stocks and shares in companies or ventures to individuals and institutions. Many individuals buy stocks and shares, collectively known as 'securities'. Many more have investments made on their behalf by the banks, building societies, pension funds and others who hold their money.

There have been major changes in recent years, brought about partly by the introduction of ICT-based systems and partly by deregulation. Trading on the floor has been replaced by trading through computer screen and telephone.

The main areas of activity for member firms of the Stock Exchange are:

- **broking (or equity sales)** – buying and selling securities on behalf of clients

- **market making (or trading)** – buying and selling securities on their own or on their firm's account

- **corporate finance** – raising finance for companies by issuing new shares

- **mergers and acquisitions** – advising client companies on merging with, or acquiring, other companies and arranging finance for such activities

- **fund management** – managing investments for institutional clients.

You may find work in any of these areas. A broker or market maker may be a firm or an individual. One individual may be a broker, market maker, or both. Firms may specialise in one or the other or in a particular market segment. Other firms offer a complete service. There are also openings to become investment analysts or researchers. These are specialists who provide market intelligence to brokers, market makers and institutional investors. You can find out more about these careers from a free booklet – *Inside Careers Guide to Banking, Securities and Investments* produced by the The Securities & Investment Institute (SII), in association with Inside Careers. You can obtain this by contacting the SII (see contact details below).

Entry qualifications

Any degree subject is acceptable, but preference is sometimes given to economics or business studies graduates. A good class degree (2.1 or better) is usually required. Those who hope to specialise as investment analysts or researchers will find that most degrees are accepted, but accountancy, economics and science are sometimes preferred. Alternatively, analysts may have degrees related to the area in which they want to specialise – surveying for property analysts, geology or chemistry for those specialising in petrochemicals. (This is obviously going to be less likely in your situation as an arts or humanities graduate.)

Regardless of which area of work you enter, you will need to be numerate, articulate and able to assimilate lots of data. You must have a good analytical mind. You should also be interested in current affairs. Above all, you must have the social skills necessary if you are to form good relationships with clients and earn their confidence.

Training and career development

You normally join your firm as a graduate trainee. A training programme of up to six months combines classroom training with on-the-job experience. The regulator for the industry – the Financial

Services Authority (FSA) – has designated a number of jobs for which you must hold an appropriate qualification. The body responsible for deciding which qualifications are acceptable for the different activities is the Financial Services Skills Council (FSSC), which publishes a list of approved qualifications. There are also some job roles, such as compliance, where the FSA requires no qualification to be held. The Securities & Investment Institute (SSI) was set up by the London Stock Exchange as the examining body for the industry and also as its professional body (with five levels of membership).

Finding vacancies

Check the annual directories (*Graduate Employment and Training (GET)* and *Prospects Directory*), which you can get free from your graduate careers service. Do consult the web. Some firms will also tell your careers service of their vacancies. And posts are also advertised in *The Financial Times*.

Further information

The London Stock Exchange – Publicity and Promotion Department, 10 Paternoster Square, London EC4M 7LS. Tel: 020 7797 1000. www.londonstockexchange.com

The Securities & Investment Institute – Centurion Street, 24 Monument Street, London EC3R 8AQ. Tel: 0207645 0600. www.sii.org.uk

Actuarial work

Actuaries calculate risks – 'the odds' of things happening. The theory of probability underlies much of this work, with the emphasis on probabilities related to living, dying, sickness and health. This differs from the work of underwriters (see Insurance earlier in this chapter), who are concerned with specific cases of insurance risk, although they use actuarial tables in their work.

Much of their work involves analysing future financial events, especially when the amount of a future payment, or the timing of when it is paid, is uncertain. About 60% of actuaries work in insurance or life assurance companies and another 30% in specialist consultancies. Some work in the Civil Service and devise public service pension schemes, inspect life assurance companies for the Department of Trade and Industry and advise on social security benefits. The Stock Exchange also employs actuaries to give investment advice to insurance companies and pension funds, based on analyses of the market.

Actuaries in life insurance

In life insurance companies, actuaries calculate the theoretical life expectancy of those buying life insurance. This varies between different groups – by age, sex (on average women live longer), occupation, state of health and other factors (on average non-smokers live longer than smokers). The actuary can then calculate rates to be charged as premiums and, as these are paid, check that the assets will cover any claims that will arise. Actuaries do similar calculations for pension schemes run by life assurance companies, trying to ensure that the premiums paid while people are working provide sufficient funds to cover their pensions from retirement until death.

The profession is relatively small, highly influential and very well paid. It is essentially a 'desk job' although those working in consultancy spend a lot of time visiting clients. The work has a high mathematical content – drawing on probability theory, compound interest calculations and a range of statistical techniques, and involves a lot of mathematical modelling on computers. However, as the results of any calculations have to be explained to non-specialists, actuaries must also communicate clearly both orally and in writing.

Entry qualifications

Although it is possible for arts and humanities graduates to go into actuarial work, most entrants to the profession have a degree in maths or a related subject. To qualify as an actuary you must register as a student member of the Institute of Actuaries (in England and Wales) or the Faculty of Actuaries (Scotland), and both these bodies require an A level at grade C in a mathematical subject (or an A grade

Higher in Scotland). This usually means that actuarial work will be of interest to only a minority of arts and humanities graduates, that is those who continued with a mathematical subject alongside their arts or humanities studies, or as part of a combined honours degree.

Training and career development

To become a qualified actuary – a Fellow of the Institute or the Faculty – requires a combination of on-the-job training and part-time study for professional examinations. In the past the examinations were notoriously difficult – with most candidates having to resit some papers. Both professional bodies say that it takes three to six years for candidates without subject exemptions to pass all their exams. The average is five years.

Tuition for the examinations is now provided for both the Institute and the Faculty by the Actuarial Education Company. Learning is through a mixture of correspondence courses and personal tuition. The Institute and the Faculty now have joint examinations. Unless you have subject exemptions, which as an arts or humanities graduate you probably won't have, you will have 17 examination papers to pass. You can only attempt an exam four times.

Your path is made easier if you can undertake a postgraduate course in actuarial science (at Cass Business School at City University, Heriot-Watt University or Kent University). This lasts one academic year (nine months) and can earn you exemptions from up to half your professional examinations. You will almost certainly have to pay for a postgraduate course yourself.

Actuaries can move out of specific actuarial work into middle and senior management, especially in life assurance companies and pension funds. There are also openings in banking, the Stock Exchange and other financial institutions.

Finding vacancies

Vacancies are advertised in *The Actuary* published monthly. Some are advertised on the shared website of the Faculty and Institute, listed below. Employers also inform the careers service of their training vacancies and advertise in the annual graduate careers directories.

Further information

The Faculty of Actuaries – MacLaurin House, 18 Dublin Street, Edinburgh EH1 3PP. Tel: 0131 240 1300.

The Institute of Actuaries – Napier House, 4 Worcester Street, Oxford OX1 2AW. Tel: 01865 268 200.

The Faculty and the Institute have a shared website, on www.actuaries.org.uk

Chapter nineteen
Careers in leisure, travel and tourism

Although these activities offer plenty of interesting openings, few posts are exclusively for graduates. You can expect to compete with non-graduates. However, you should find that the transferable skills acquired during your degree studies give you a distinct advantage.

Arts administrator

Arts administrators perform a similar function to producers working in the theatre. They organise events such as concerts and plays, usually in publicly owned venues. The responsibilities include:

- planning seasonal programmes

- organising individual events

- booking venues

- engaging performers

- publicity

- handling ticket sales

- negotiating grants from public funds and commercial sponsorship

- day-to-day administration.

Employers are often local authorities working alone or together with private industry. Alternatively, you might work directly for a theatre or theatre company. The exact nature of your job will depend largely on the size of the organisation for which you work. For example, in a large theatre company you might specialise in marketing, whereas at a small local theatre you would be responsible for all administrative support.

Entry qualifications

If you want to become an arts administrator in the public sector, you'd be wise to study part time for the Diploma of the Institute of Leisure and Amenity Management as soon as you can after starting the job. As a graduate you should be exempt from some of the papers. Local authorities are very conscious of the value of qualifications, and your progress may be limited if you don't get the relevant pieces of paper.

Charlene McManus

Charlene, 23, has managed to achieve her ambition of working in a specialist area of arts administration – working in an agency representing performers and entertainers.

Career profile

Job title: agent's assistant

Employer: RDF Management

A Levels: drama, psychology, English

Degree: BA performing arts and arts management (Hons).

University: De Montfort, Leicester

'I did A level drama at school because I've always been interested in it – not necessarily to act but just to find out how it all works. I was interested in psychology, but we didn't do it at school, so I did it as an evening course. And I've always enjoyed English.

At uni I did a joint honours degree in performing arts and arts management. I did them together so I could get both the managing side and the performing arts side. I wanted to see how it works from both sides. I did a few work placements as part of my course, one in a recording studio and another in a theatre.

I've always wanted to be an agent since I was at school, but I never thought I'd get into it. It was an ambition, but not necessarily something I thought I could do. So when I left uni I temped for about a year doing various admin jobs while I worked out what I wanted to do. I thought I needed to get some people and admin skills. So I worked for the Council and also the Crown Prosecution Service. Then I met up with a friend of my sister, who worked for a magazine and gave me some contact names in agencies.

I sent my CV off to various agents and asked if they wanted me to do any work experience for them. I got a response from RDF Management. They're a specialist agency representing actors, writers, presenters and stand-up comedians. They took me on for two weeks' work experience, paying me just for travel and lunch expenses. They then kept me on for another month as a paid member of staff, just helping out as a junior. Then a girl already working there decided to leave and I was asked if I wanted the vacancy as a junior, which I did. Now I've been made an agent's assistant.

The placements we did at uni were helpful to me in the job, because we were able to go into theatre and music companies. Most of our work was around case studies and real places in the area around Leicester. We analysed real companies. So we would take a theatre and ask, what does it need to do? What marketing strategies does it have? It was a really good course to do.

I have been quite lucky, because my manager went off on maternity leave quite recently. I've been in the job for a year, and after only six months she went off leaving me and another colleague to look after her clients. As my manager is the head of the agency, there was real mix of clients – actors, presenters and comedians. So I was thrown in the deep end. But it's been really good for me because there were some things I wouldn't have been able to do otherwise. For instance, I've been able to negotiate money and deal with contracts. These are things that I would normally be able to do only a long way down the line. A lot of companies don't give you the responsibility that quickly, so I have been lucky.

My manager is back now. It's going well because she knows what I am capable of doing. She was happy with the way things went and nothing went wrong, which was good! I think it's sometimes good to be thrown in at the deep end to either sink or swim!

During my course I found this to be quite a laid-back industry. And being at university and having done drama you get a lot more confidence to meet people and talk to them. And I learned the computer skills that I'm using now.

I'd advise anyone thinking of taking an arts or humanities degree to research it a lot. There are so many choices that you may overlook something you really want to do. I never thought arts management even existed – but when I saw it I knew instantly it was what I wanted to do. It was perfect for me.

I'd also advise people to get some work experience. We were lucky, because it was part of our course. I think it is always a good thing to use your time at uni to do at least a month's work experience in your chosen field. It shows potential employers that you are keen, and that is a massive factor.'

Conference and exhibition manager

Exhibition and conference centres, and some larger hotels, employ managers to organise and direct all the appropriate services for the running of events. These can range from one-day events involving a few dozen delegates to events attended by several thousand people over three or four days. The latter may combine an exhibition with a programme of lectures and meetings, which may be held in several halls simultaneously.

The manager will have overall responsibility for ensuring that all the services run smoothly – exhibition stands, delegate reception, accommodation and catering, lecture rooms and their seating, audio-visual equipment, press office, entertainment and so on. The manager, obviously, will be leading a team of people, but he or she will be responsible for all the planning and ensuring that the customer is happy, that everything runs smoothly (or that any problems are solved satisfactorily as they arise) and that the event is profitable.

Employers usually look for a few years' prior experience in the hotel, catering or tourism industries.

Entertainments officer

The work involves keeping your company's guests or passengers happy with a range of entertainments, from games nights to stage shows. As an entertainments officer you will perform a range of duties including socialising with the guests, compèring shows and taking part in performances. There may be opportunities to progress into management, running the entertainments programmes for a leisure operation. A degree in the performing arts could be an asset but certainly would not be essential.

Hotel manager

As a hotel manager you would be responsible for running every aspect of a hotel. This is likely to include organising the furnishing, maintenance and cleaning of bedroom accommodation and all public areas; the running of the restaurant, bars and the reception area; greeting new guests and dealing with customer complaints; and, above all, being responsible for the financial performance of the business.

In a large hotel you would have a management team with several heads of departments. In a small hotel you would carry out all the management tasks and even give a helping hand if any staff were absent.

Some of the larger hotel groups offer graduate training programmes that last one to two years and lead to head of department posts or to assistant manager on completion. In smaller hotels the training tends to be far more haphazard and you learn on the job.

Catering manager

Catering managers are employed in hotels, restaurants, works canteens, hospitals and care homes, cruise liners, schools, conference centres, the Houses and Parliament and other places where large numbers of people need to eat and drink. They have to plan, organise and manage the food and beverage services. They have to achieve customer satisfaction while balancing quality and cost. They are also responsible for maintaining high standards of cleanliness and food hygiene.

Most graduates who go into catering have experience of doing part-time or seasonal jobs in pubs, restaurants and fast-food outlets at weekends and during university vacations. Unless you have a relevant degree you're probably best starting on a 'graduate apprenticeship'. This normally takes a year and consists of work-based training that leads to a relevant qualification.

Travel industry

'All travel has its advantages. If the passenger visits better countries, he may learn to improve his own. And if fortune carries him to worse, he may learn to enjoy it.'

Dr Samuel Johnson, writer and lexicographer

The travel industry has a glamorous image but offers few opportunities for graduates. There are some 5000 travel agents who sell a variety of travel and tour packages. Entry is usually as a clerk, the vast majority of whom join without any higher education. There is also a high proportion of junior to senior staff, so promotion prospects are not very good.

If you want to satisfy the travel bug, and you have language skills, you might choose to be a travel courier for a season or two. However, you cannot make a career from such jobs alone. You should also be aware that you may find it more difficult to enter a career with a permanent employer afterwards.

As a courier you look after business or holiday travellers, usually while travelling by luxury coach but sometimes by train, plane or car.

You care for your party throughout the trip – welcome them, give a commentary on places of interest during the tour, liaise with hotels and restaurants, and generally ensure that your clients have a trouble-free and enjoyable trip.

Couriers must communicate well, get on with people and remain calm under pressure. Few trips are trouble free. Couriers have to deal with a range of problems as they arise – lost luggage, overbooked hotels, late arrivals, medical emergencies, and so on. The work isn't well paid, but you get the same standard of food and accommodation as your clients. In practice you're rarely off-duty on tour. Even so, competition for these posts is fierce.

Resort representatives work for tour operators. They do similar work to couriers but are based in a resort, where they are likely to look after clients in several hotels. Many are on short-term contracts and are employed by the season. They often move into administration and management at headquarters.

With regard to longer-term opportunities, tour operators offer the best chances for graduates, but they are few in number. The larger companies have well-established graduate training schemes. Vacancies are mainly in marketing, information technology, contracting and finance.

As a contractor you would have to negotiate with airlines, coach companies, hotels and villa owners getting the best possible prices for your company. Finance is also critical to the success of a travel company, because profit margins are normally very low for package holidays and budgets must be monitored very closely. Moreover, companies often have to buy foreign currency to meet future needs in case the pound loses value. It takes considerable judgement (and some luck) to anticipate what exchange rates are going to do. (See information on accountancy, Chapter eighteen).

Although you are likely to spend a few weeks abroad during training, these careers do not offer many travel opportunities other than the chance of cheap holidays as a 'perk'. As one graduate recruitment brochure puts it: 'If your main interest is travelling or using foreign languages, you should not apply to this scheme.'

'Travel is glamorous only in retrospect.'

Paul Theroux, American writer

Tourism officer

Tourism officers are responsible for marketing the attractions of a particular region or tourist attraction with the aim of increasing visitor numbers. This would involve you in running visitor services, such as a tourist office, and dealing with enquiries from both the public and those providing visitor services, such as tourist attractions, hotels and tour operators. You would be responsible for strategic planning and organising new attractions, festivals, fairs and other events to attract visitors. This would involve liaising with local officials and relevant organisations and could also involve you in fund raising. You would also be involved in producing literature for visitors, running a website, writing press releases, and possibly involved in video and television commercials.

On the administrative side you would also be managing and motivating your staff, and writing and presenting reports for your employer. Your employer could be local government or another public body, or you may work for a private organisation that owns a major tourist attraction.

You could well have a relevant degree (perhaps in tourism, marketing, journalism or, if your area gets lots of overseas visitors, modern languages), although this is not essential.

Further information

The Hotel and Catering International Management Association – Trinity Court, 34 West Street Sutton, Surrey SM1 1SH. Tel: 020 8661 4900. The professional body for hospitality, leisure and tourism professionals. www.hcima.org.uk

Springboard UK – 3 Denmark Street, London WC2H 8LP. Tel: 020 7497 8654. Promotes hospitality, leisure, travel and tourism careers, and produces a range of careers information. www.springboarduk.org.uk

Chapter twenty
Other options

Even in a book of this size it's impossible to describe adequately every career open to an arts or humanities graduate. This book has sought to describe some of the mainstream choices. There are many more options, and a few of the more important ones are briefly described in this chapter. But you should realise that if none of the careers in this book appeals to you, there are still many others to consider. Do some research – and don't just look at the obvious.

Computing, information technology and management services

For some years, only computer specialists understood and ran the technology and programmes. End-users had to employ these specialists to run their computer systems. But as computing capacity has grown, applications have increased, costs have fallen and systems have become much more user-friendly. Computing is now a normal part of most business. Those employed in computing, with the exception of those who design computers and software, no longer need to be technical specialists. Today's operator may be anyone – student, consulting engineer, nurse, author, business manager, scientist, shopkeeper or teacher.

These changes have altered the type of person employers look for. In many areas of computing – increasingly called IT or management services – your computing skills are no more important than your knowledge of the business. Many employers recruit generalists rather than specialists and train them as required, giving them a knowledge of the business combined with computing skills.

The most likely area of work for arts and humanities graduates is systems analysis/programming. As an analyst you work with the end-users of the system to find out exactly what they need it to do for them. You adapt existing software, or create new programs, to make the system work.

Entry qualifications

To be a systems analyst/programmer you must have an analytical mind, commercial awareness and the ability to communicate clearly with non-specialists.

Of all employers who advertise computing and management services posts, around half accept any degree discipline. Others state a preference for specific degrees but still welcome arts and humanities graduates. For example, IBM says: 'We recruit from a wide range of degree disciplines. Although degrees with an element of computing experience are relevant for the more technical positions, many arts graduates prove to be just as successful in these areas.'

There is a widening gap between technical specialists and generalists in computing. A growing number of generalists already make computing only a part of their career, and then progress into other areas of management.

Retailing

Retailing used to have a poor image among graduates. This was not helped by experiences of Saturday jobs, filling the shelves in a local supermarket. This gives a totally false impression of the jobs that graduates do in retailing. The larger retailing operations now offer very interesting challenges in a variety of jobs such as finance, quality assurance, marketing, buying and merchandising. Some of these functions are described in Chapter seventeen. The more successful retailers run very sophisticated operations using the latest systems and technology, especially IT. The main openings are in store management.

Most vacancies are in supermarkets, multiples (chain stores specialising in such areas as electrical goods, books and CDs, outdoor sports, furniture and fashion) and departmental stores. Don't choose a retailer just because you like the products – such as CDs, fashion clothes or software. Choose one with a good training programme, a reputation for long-term success and good staff relations. Among those you might consider are the John Lewis Partnership (including Waitrose), W H Smith, Morrisons, Sainsbury's and Tesco. A graduate joining a large group could be managing a supermarket with a turnover of around £1 million a week and be earning £40,000 a year before they are 30 years old.

Although most retailers stick to normal day-time opening, others now stay open in the evenings (some to 10pm), while some supermarkets are now open 24 hours a day for seven days a week. Consequently, shift working and unsocial hours are often the price you have to pay for a high salary and good career opportunities.

Unlike most careers, you can sample what different retailers are like by visiting their stores. Watch how they deal with customers, talk to people working there, and if you're really keen, ask to meet some management staff.

Legal work

Barristers and solicitors are both legal professionals, which it is possible to train for after completing an arts or humanities degree.

Barristers work in the courts defending and prosecuting cases referred to them by solicitors. They may also represent clients at public enquiries. Some barristers work as legal advisers and consultants. QCs (Queen's Councils) and judges are selected from the ranks of barristers. Most barristers are self-employed, and work in chambers (offices). There are also employed opportunities, working for the Crown Prosecution Service and in the Government Legal Service.

Solicitors have day-to-day contact with the public, giving advice on all kinds of legal matters. They represent clients in the county courts and magistrates' courts (and, in certain circumstances, in the higher courts). Solicitors give instructions to barristers for the cases which barristers present in court. Solicitors usually specialise in areas like property sale and purchase, company law, family law or criminal law. Solicitors work in private practice, commerce and industry and for local government and the Civil Service, including the Crown Prosecution Service and the Government Legal Service.

Training

To become a barrister, non-law graduates (who need at least a second class honours degree) must take a one-year, full-time (or two-year, part-time) conversion course. This is followed by taking the Bar Vocational Course – one-year, full-time or two-year, part-time. Then you have to find a year's pupillage with an experienced barrister. After that, you apply for a tenancy or for an employed position. Competition is stiff at all stages of the training.

To train as a solicitor, non-law graduates must take a conversion course, as described above. This must be followed by the Legal Practice Course (one-year, full-time or two-year, part-time) and finally, you must find a two-year training contract in a solicitor's office or other approved organisation. There is great competition for training contract positions.

For more information, visit the following websites:
www.barcouncil.org.uk
www.legaleducation.org.uk

www.lawsociety.org.uk
www.lcan.org.uk

Self-employment

Many of us, at one time or another, want to run our own business and be our own boss. In the past ten years the number of self-employed people in the UK has gone up by a million to three-and-a-quarter million. It is expected that an increasing part of the workforce will become self-employed in the years ahead. However, many of these people will not run their own businesses in the usual sense but do contract work for employers. It's true that some newly qualified graduates have started their own businesses and prospered, but they are in a minority. A high proportion of new businesses – even when they are started by experienced managers – fail. Recent research suggests that the younger you are, the greater the risk of failure.

'If a man... make a better mousetrap than his neighbour, though he build his house in the woods, the world will make a beaten path to his door.'

Ralph Waldo Emerson, American author, poet and philosopher

Sadly, these well-known words of wisdom have proved to be false. It's not enough to have a first-class idea for a new or better product or service. You must also know how to market it. If you get your marketing wrong, you'll almost certainly fail. You'll also find there is far more administrative work than you might at first imagine – a lot of it to satisfy the taxman, and 'vatman' in HM Customs and Excise and the law. People setting up new businesses often vastly underestimate the amount of money they need to survive the first few months and may fail because of this misconception.

It is better to learn some basic marketing, administrative, financial and other skills before you set up your business. For your first few years, at least, you are likely to be working almost all your waking hours – including weekends. This is not the time to learn the basic skills you'll need. So, if it's your firm ambition to start your own business, you should get a few years' work experience and learn as much as possible while earning some capital. The single most useful function to learn is marketing, but working in any commercial function is valuable. While you are in work you should try and learn how the business operates as a whole. Study how the various functions interlink and are mutually dependent.

You should make a particular point of learning how the business:

■ identifies the needs of its customers and potential customers

■ tailors its products, and its level of service, to customer needs

■ provides prompt deliveries without holding too much stock

■ maintains a high and consistent standard of quality and service

■ handles customer complaints

■ communicates with its customers and potential customers

■ uses marketing, financial and other information to make decisions

■ motivates and develops the skills of its employees

■ obtains good service from its suppliers

■ ensures that its customers pay promptly.

Because any new business starts on a small scale, you may think it best to gain experience in a small company. However, these rarely offer formal training or the quality of experience you need. You'll probably learn more from a structured training programme with a big employer. The business principles are the same whether you are in a large or small firm.

You must be just as well prepared if you plan to work as a freelance, offering your talents as an individual rather than setting up a firm. You must be sure that you have sufficient expertise in the line of work you intend to follow. If at all possible, test the water by doing some freelance work before you leave your full-time job, and see if you can start to develop a portfolio of clients.

Starting a business is always a risk – but the potential rewards are high. By preparing yourself well, you can cut the risk of failure substantially. In addition to the commercial awareness and abilities that you have developed in employment, there are a number of personal qualities that are essential. You'll need to have good communication skills (including listening skills), to be well organised (especially in the way you handle any paperwork) and to be able to manage your time effectively. You must have good negotiating skills, and both physical and mental stamina. Just about every business goes through difficult periods, especially in its early days. You'll need both single-minded determination and unquenchable enthusiasm to see you through.

Further information

Your careers service will have some information about self-employment, but you will probably find it extremely helpful to ask your bank for any guide it produces on starting a business or becoming self-employed. There are also a number of books available, which detail both the practical and personal considerations. Some include self-assessment questionnaires that will help you to evaluate whether or not you are likely to be suited to self-employment.

Conclusion

As I hope you have gathered from this book, few doors are closed to arts or humanities graduates. Science and technology will have little for you, and in view of your subject choice you probably aren't that interested. But even here there are occasional opportunities. For example, the BBC used to take on arts or humanities graduates and train them to degree-level standard in electronic engineering. This has enabled them to do equal work and hold equal status in the BBC as graduate engineers.

Whatever decision you make regarding your career, it is vital that you make it at least one full year before you leave university. If you do not (and many students don't) you will substantially reduce your chances of finding a graduate-level job.

'When you have to make a choice and don't make it, that is in itself a choice.'

William Joyce, Nazi propagandist

Section 4

Sources of advice
and information

You face a bewildering choice of educational and career options, and making a decision that's right for you will not be easy. Fortunately, there is a lot of help available. The more information and advice you can get, the less chance there is that you will make a poor decision.

Chapter twenty-one looks at the many people who can give you helpful advice. But don't lose sight of the fact that the quality of advice can vary, so never rely on just one source. Chapter twenty-two also provides a list of book and website sources that you should find helpful.

Remember that however many people advise you, and however many books and websites you use, the final decision must always be yours. The educational and career choices you make now will largely determine what kind of life you'll enjoy in the years ahead. You can't let someone else, however well meaning they are, make these choices for you.

Chapter twenty-one
Sources of advice

You're probably already receiving a lot of advice about your future – whether you want it or not. It may be coming from friends of your own age, family and friends of the family, and teachers. Don't ignore the advice, even if you may choose to reject it later. It's always worth listening.

'Advice is seldom welcome; and those who need it the most always want it the least.'

Earl of Chesterfield

You should also actively seek advice – from your careers teacher, from the careers/Connexions service and so on. Obviously, it's helpful to know how much trust you can put in each source. This chapter looks at some possible sources of advice and information, and how each of them may be useful.

Friends

Most of us find it easiest to relate to people of our own age. To discuss your hopes and likes and dislikes with friends, and exchange information and ideas, can help to clarify your thinking. Friends can also help you to see aspects of your character that might make you unsuited to some types of work, or draw your attention to strengths that you hadn't considered. All this is helpful. But, they're not likely to have any more experience of university or working life than you. Nor are their ideas on specific careers likely to be any more reliable than your own.

Family

Parents and other relatives, and adult family friends, will want to help you to make the right decisions. They can give you lots of sound advice based on their practical experience. However, you and they need to understand that both the world of education and the world of work have changed enormously since they were your age. So you both need to be aware that their experience will not apply to you directly.

When your parents were your age, only one in ten people went into higher education – now approaching half do so. The status of graduates has changed a lot since they left university. Employers have different expectations of graduates and no longer see them as an elite. Most of those graduating with a first degree have the status that a bright school-leaver with five good 'O' levels enjoyed 25 years ago. A first degree is becoming the basic entry qualification for 'white collar' work.

Parents and other adults can give useful factual information about the careers they're in. Ask them the purpose of what they do, the tasks they undertake day to day, how they do them, and what skills they are using. What do they most like and dislike about their work? What training did they receive? How is their career developing? And what do they and their employers do to keep their knowledge and skills up to date?

However, don't forget that people's opinions can be coloured by particularly good or bad experiences at work. While you can normally rely on the factual information you are given, treat opinions with some caution.

Make your decisions

Be aware that people of all ages have lots of misconceptions about other people's jobs. Except for careers specialists, people are not a reliable source of factual information on careers outside their own immediate experience.

Your parents and adult relatives should understand that careers, which are attractive to them, may hold no interest for you – and vice versa. If a parent has found great satisfaction in a particular career, it is understandable if they try to persuade you to follow in their footsteps.

On the other hand, some parents who were unable to follow their own ambitions want to give their children the chance to do what they never could. In either case, you're unlikely to share those same career ambitions. Young people are not clones of their parents but unique individuals with their own set of abilities and preferences.

Work-shadowing

If any adults, relatives or friends work in areas of interest to you, ask if there is any possibility of 'work-shadowing' them for a typical day or week during your holidays. Adult relatives or friends may also know people working in career areas that interest you. They may be able to arrange for you to talk to them, visit their workplace, or even 'shadow' them at work through a typical day or few days during your holidays. This experience can be invaluable, particularly if you ask intelligent questions. The fact that you have done some work-shadowing is also valued by university admissions officers and by prospective employers.

Teachers

Your teachers can guide you on your educational choices. This doesn't mean they'll be familiar with all the degree courses that may interest you – the choice is too great and changes too frequently. What they can do is indicate the subject areas in which you're likely to do well or badly. There's not much point wanting to study classical archaeology, for example, if you have difficulty with Latin or ancient Greek. Teachers can help you to focus your choices by identifying your strengths and weaknesses.

On the other hand, most of your teachers are no better placed than anyone else to give you reliable information about careers outside teaching. At times, you actually need to be cautious of how teachers relate your schoolwork to your career ambitions. Teachers are not always fully aware of what a particular career entails or what skills are required. For example, perhaps you want to become a journalist – your teacher may try to discourage you by saying, with perfect accuracy, that your creative writing is pedestrian and lacking in imagination.

But journalism doesn't involve creative writing – it is concerned with gathering and analysing information and presenting it clearly and succinctly. Similarly, a teacher may deter you from accountancy or banking because your maths is weak, not realising that maths is much less important than communication and interpersonal skills.

Careers teachers

While several of your teachers may be involved in 'careers education' of one sort or another, one will be responsible for keeping, updating and managing a central collection of careers literature, videos and learning packages. This teacher, although not a careers specialist, can help you with lots of information about degree courses and about careers. Your school may also provide opportunities for you to attend talks from employers, and to shadow people at work for a day or two. All state schools should organise a period of 'worthwhile work experience' for their students. Some schools even arrange holiday work experience. You should use these opportunities and learn as much as you can.

Personal advisers and careers advisers

Professional personal advisers and careers advisers normally provide the most objective and reliable careers information. In England, personal advisers work for Connexions services, which provide advice and guidance for 13- to 19-year-olds, not only on careers but also advice on other personal issues. In other parts of the UK careers advisers work in local careers services (in Scotland these are run by Careers Scotland, and in Wales by Careers Wales). Your careers teacher will be able to tell you about your local service.

Wherever they work, such advisers are highly trained professionals. As well as being very knowledgeable, they have access to good sources of up-to-date information. The local Connexions/careers service will normally send an adviser regularly into each school. They give what they call 'non-directive' counselling, discussing and clarifying the options available. In other words, they're not there to tell you what you should do or what you are best suited to do. Their job is to help you to make your own decision by helping you to find out what you need to know.

Apart from any school visits they make, they can also be consulted outside school hours. You can take your parents or guardian with you if you wish, and this can often be helpful. You may need to make an appointment to see an adviser, but the service is free.

Psychometric and aptitude tests

In Chapter two (page 25), self-assessment tests are mentioned. These can help you determine where your interests and aptitudes lie and so give you some ideas about suitable study and career choices. Your careers teacher or local personal/careers adviser may have psychometric or aptitude tests available that you can take free of charge. There are also books of aptitude tests that you can work through on your own. Probably the best is *Test Your Own Aptitude* (3rd edition), published by Kogan Page, £8.99. This is written by two occupational psychologists with lots of experience of careers counselling.

However, the best way to have your interests, aptitudes and personality tested is through a qualified chartered occupational psychologist. Not only will they use carefully designed tests, but they will discuss the findings and their implications with you in detail.

Occupational psychologists

If you really don't know what you want to do, you could spend a day undergoing assessment and counselling with an occupational psychologist. Although quite expensive (typically £375-425) this can be a good investment. You will take a battery of psychometric tests that look at your interests (the things you like and dislike doing), your aptitudes (what you are likely to be good at doing) and your personality (the sort of person you are). These have no right or wrong answers. If you're faced with such tests (and employers use them regularly during graduate selection) it is important in your own interest to answer them honestly.

Using the information provided by the tests, the occupational psychologist will then explore with you a range of options – some of which may not have occurred to you before. Finally, you will be sent a written report.

Do not expect to be told that you are ideally suited to a particular career. Rather it will be a matter of narrowing the range of your options, and making sure you are aware of others to which you are suited but which you might not have considered. The decision still rests with you. However, don't forget that the interest questionnaires that you complete now draw on your current knowledge and experience. In another few years, especially if you are not yet at university, you'll have learned a lot more about yourself and the options available to you. You will find that you have developed a range of new interests. So keep some flexibility in your plans.

If you decide to consult a psychologist, be aware that not everybody offering testing and careers counselling on a commercial basis is qualified to do so. You should only consult a chartered occupational psychologist on the register of the British Psychological Society (BPS). You will find a list of these on the Society's website at www.bps.org. uk (click on 'find a psychologist' then on 'The Directory of Chartered Psychologists'). And if you want to check that someone offering testing and careers counselling services is qualified to do so, go to the same BPS website, click on 'find a psychologist' and then on 'The Register of Chartered Psychologists'.

University careers advisory service

Once you are at university your most reliable source of careers advice is the careers advisory service. It provides a very wide range of services. Among them are:

- giving individual students objective counselling

- maintaining large careers libraries (including files on all the major graduate employers)

- distributing a mass of free literature (such as careers directories, employers' recruitment brochures and job application forms)

- organising talks on specific careers, job applications, interview techniques and other topics

- running careers information fairs and recruitment fairs

- organising presentations by employers

- arranging 'milkround' visits by recruiters, including organising interviews for students

- keeping up-to-date details of job vacancies sent in by employers

- helping students find vacation work and other work experience opportunities.

Services differ a little in the way they operate, but the principles are the same. You should seek individual counselling in your second year. In the first term of your final year you will be able to consult the new editions of the careers directories. These are published annually and give detailed information on employers and their requirements. The two main directories are:

- *Graduate Employment and Training* (usually just called GET), published by Hobsons.

- *Prospects Directory*, published by the commercial arm of the Higher Education Careers Service Unit.

Both have online versions: www.get.hobsons.co.uk and www.prospects. ac.uk

Publishers' addresses and details of other useful books are given in Chapter twenty-two.

After consulting the directories, get copies of the recruitment brochures of any organisations that appeal to you. It is worth checking the websites of these employers for any updated information (including new vacancies). You could also consult the employer files kept by your careers service. Individual files are kept for each employer, and these are likely to contain the current recruitment brochure, press cuttings and articles, details of recent vacancies, salaries and much else. Also try to attend employer presentations, information fairs and careers workshops.

Start applying to employers in your final year. Although fewer employers use the milkround than in the past, those who recruit large numbers, and particularly those who seek 'high-flying' management trainees, still do so. Milkround recruiters usually have an application deadline – often pre-Christmas. Your careers service will have closing dates for applications. This is probably the best opportunity you will have for graduate-level employment.

Students often delay contacting their careers service. One in three undergraduates don't make any applications until after sitting their finals. But by then, many if not most of the most attractive vacancies are already filled. Don't delay visiting your careers service and don't leave your applications too late. It is worth noting that an *Early Bird* research report, by occupational psychologists SHL, in 2005, found that graduates who apply earlier for jobs are likely to be brighter than their peers and have a greater chance of success in the workplace. Those who apply later were found to be more resilient but less forward thinking, less analytical, less motivated, less outgoing and less persuasive. The late applicants probably need their greater resilience!

Chapter twenty-two
Sources of information

This chapter lists books and websites that may be helpful to you in choosing a degree course, finding information on specific careers and finding an employer. Many of them can be found in your school or graduate careers advisory service, in your public library or by accessing the relevant websites. Otherwise, you could order and buy books through a good bookshop, online or from the publisher (see the addresses at the end of the chapter). Always use the latest editions because information is soon out of date.

General

Student Life: a survival guide published by Lifetime Careers Publishing, £10.99. A survival guide for anyone beginning, or soon to begin, university or college.

Decisions at 17/18+ published by Lifetime Careers Publishing in association with CRAC, £10.99. A student helpbook looking at the full range of choices at 18 – higher education and employment.

Degree course choice

University and College Entrance: The Official Guide (annual) published by The Universities and Colleges Admissions Service (UCAS), £32.50 (book and CD-ROM) or £15 (CD-ROM only). The 'Big Guide' provides details of all UK degree and HND courses at publicly funded institutions.

Which Degree (Volume 1) (annual) published by Hobsons together with the Careers Research and Advisory Centre (CRAC), £24.99. Covers UK arts, humanities, languages, social sciences, business, education and law courses. Divided into subject chapters, with courses arranged alphabetically by title and institution.

Green Guides published by Trotman, £9.99. Annual books in this new series include comprehensive and up-to-date listings of all degree courses, profiles of institutions and case studies. Copies should be available in your school careers library. The arts and humanities titles are:

- *Creative Arts Courses*

- *Business Courses.*

CRAC *Degree Course Guides* published by Trotman, £9.99. Describe the content and character of each course. Arts and humanities titles cover:

- *Art and Design, History of Art and Design*

- *Business and Economics*

- *Classics, Theology and Religious Studies*

- *English, Media Studies and American Studies*

- *History, Archaeology and Politics*

- *Hospitality, Leisure and Tourism*

- *Modern Languages and European Studies*

- *Music, Drama and Dance*

- *Psychology, Philosophy and Linguistics.*

Degree Course Offers (annual, May) published by Trotman, £26.99 (paperback). Lists all first degree courses, detailing grade and points requirements, what admissions tutors look for, and gives typical interview questions.

Choosing Your Degree Course and University (biennial, March) published by Trotman, £21.99. Practical advice on how to select the right course and university; includes data on the relative quality of courses.

The Times Good University Guide 2006 published by Times Books, £15.99 (discounted by *The Times*, Amazon, etc). Profiles each British university with league tables showing the strengths and weaknesses of each; offers advice on choosing and applying for the best course for you.

How to Complete Your UCAS Application (17th edition) published by Trotman. This useful volume helps you to apply for courses through UCAS. It takes you through the whole application process, giving all the essential dos and don'ts, as well as providing guidance on the very important 'personal statement'.

'Course Discover' – you might also want to consult this online resource. Working in partnership with over 1,000 UK and Irish universities and colleges, this lists more than 120,000 courses and gives details of course content, entry requirements, accommodation costs, disabled facilities, open day dates and much more. If your school subscribes to this subscription-only service, you can consult it at home as well as at school. The website is at www.coursediscover.co.uk

Careers

If you are not yet sure which career area interests you most, several books describe a wide range of careers with their entry requirements, training, etc. Two of the most up to date are:

The Times A–Z of Careers and Jobs (12th edition) published by Kogan Page, £14.99.

The Penguin Careers Guide (12th edition) published by Penguin, £12.99.

The 'jobs4u' careers database is a comprehensive guide – available on the Connexions website. This covers virtually every type of job (manual to professional) with a description of the work, work environment, entry requirements, training, prospects, and pay and conditions. www.connexions-direct.com/jobs4u

The *GET* series (annual series formerly known as *Hobsons Casebooks*) available from Trotman. Each book reviews a career area in which graduates with a wide variety of employers describe their work experiences. Available free from university careers services. Careers with some openings for arts and humanities graduates are:

- *Finance*
- *Science and IT*
- *Law*
- *Management.*

'Explore types of jobs' – a very useful resource provided by Prospects on behalf of The Association of Graduate Careers Advisory Services (AGCAS). This provides up-to-date and detailed information on a huge range of graduate-level jobs, including entry requirements and training. Click on 'Jobs and work', then 'Explore types of jobs' on www.prospects.ac.uk

Inside Careers guides (annual series) published by Inside Careers in partnership with the appropriate professional institutions, £10 each. Contents can be read and downloaded as pdf files free on www. insidecareers.co.uk The titles that may be of interest to arts and humanities graduates are:

- *Actuaries*
- *Banking, Securities and Investment*
- *Chartered Accountants*
- *Information Technology*
- *Logistics and Transport Management*
- *Management Consultancy*
- *The Chartered Tax Advisers Profession.*

A popular and inexpensive, but in some cases dated, series of paperback careers books is the *Careers in* guides published by Kogan Page, £8.99 unless otherwise shown. Unlike the AGCAS and Inside Careers titles, these are not aimed specifically at graduates but at a wider audience. Relevant titles are:

- *Careers in Accountancy* (seventh edition)
- *Careers in Art and Design* (eighth edition)

- *Careers in Catering, Hotel Administration and Management* (sixth edition) (£9.99)

- *Careers Using English* (£9.99)

- *Careers in Fashion* (fifth edition)

- *Careers in Film and Video* (fifth edition) (£7.99)

- *Careers in Human Resource Management*

- *Careers in Journalism* (eighth edition)

- *Careers Using Languages* (eighth edition) (£9.99)

- *Careers in Marketing, Advertising and Public Relations* (eighth edition) (£9.99)

- *Careers in Music Careers in the Police Service* (sixth edition) (£9.99)

- *Careers in Retailing* (sixth edition)

- *Careers in Teaching* (seventh edition)

- *Careers in Television and Radio* (seventh edition)

- *Careers in the Theatre* (sixth edition).

The *Insider Careers Guides* published by Spiro Press, £9.99 each is a similar, but also dated, series, and includes:

- *Advertising, Marketing and PR*

- *Banking and the City*

- *Broadcasting and the Media*

- *Information and Communications Technology*

- *Retailing*

- *Travel and Tourism.*

Choosing an employer

The following directories are available free on campus to final year undergraduates. As well as advice on job search, they contain detailed employer entries describing the vacancies on offer, the type of work, training schemes, locations and much more.

Graduate Employment and Training (commonly known as GET) published annually by Hobsons together with CRAC.

Prospects Directory published annually by CSU for the Association of Graduate Careers Advisory Services.

Also published by CSU:

- *Prospects Today* is a fortnightly jobs and careers magazine issued between April and June

- *Prospects Finalist* contains vacancies for final-year students; published five times a year (October to May)

- *Prospects Graduate* a recent addition to the CSU stable; a digital magazine distributed fortnightly by email; carries online advertising.

If you seek a graduate career elsewhere in Europe, there are several similar annual directories. The following are among those that may be available in your graduate careers advisory service:

- Belgium, *Move-up*

- France, *Go Editions*

- The Netherlands, *Intermediair Jaarboek*

- Spain, *Guia de las Empresas que Ofrecen Empleo*.

Your careers service may also have the series of leaflets, published by Careers Europe, on working in different EU member states.

Publishers

All publication enquiries and orders should be addressed to the relevant publishers below. Please note all the prices quoted above are those current in September 2005.

Connexions Service National Unit – DfES Publications, PO Box 99, Sudbury, Suffolk CO10 2SN. Tel: 0845 602 2260. www.connexions.gov.uk

CSU Ltd – Prospects House, Booth Street East, Manchester M13 9EP. Tel: 0161 277 5200. www.prospects.ac.uk

Hobsons plc – Hobsons Customer Services, c/o NBN International, Estover Road, Plymouth, Devon PL6 7PZ. Tel:020 7958 5000. www.hobsons.com

Inside Careers – The Quadrangle, 49 Atalanta Street, London SW6 6TR. Tel: 020 7565 7900. www.insidecareers.co.uk

Kogan Page Ltd – 120 Pentonville Road, London N1 9JN. Tel: 020 7278 0433. www.kogan-page.co.uk

Lifetime Careers Publishing – c/o Orca Book Services Ltd, Stanley House, 3 Fleets Lane, Poole, Dorset BH15 3AJ. Tel: 01202 665432. www.lifetime-publishing.co.uk

Spiro Press – Quadrant Court, 49 Calthorpe Road, Edgbaston, Birmingham B15 1TH. Tel: 0870 400 1099. www.spiropress.com

Trotman & Co Ltd – c/o NBN International, Estover Road, Plymouth, Devon PL6 7PY. Tel: 0870 900 2665. www.trotman.co.uk

The Universities and Colleges Admissions Service (UCAS) – Rosehill, New Barn Lane, Cheltenham, Gloucestershire GL52 3LZ. Tel: 01242 227788. www.ucas.com

Index

More titles in the Student Helpbook series ...

helping students of all ages make the right choices about their careers and education.

New edition
Careers with a Science Degree
Published in association with UCAS
An excellent read for anyone considering science at degree level.
£10.99   ISBN: 1 904979 07 6

A Year Off ... A Year On?
Published in association with UCAS
All the information and advice you need on how to make the most of your time out between courses or jobs.
£10.99   ISBN: 1 902876 86 5

New edition
Student Life: A Survival Guide
Published in association with UCAS
Essential advice for students beginning or soon to begin university or college; includes invaluable help on how to budget and get the most out of their time.
£10.99   ISBN: 1 904979 01 7

Jobs and Careers after A levels and equivalent advanced qualifications
Opportunities for students leaving school or college at 18, including advice on job-hunting, applications and interviews.
£10.99   ISBN: 1 902876 93 8

CVs and Applications
For anyone who is applying for a job or college place; includes details of how to use the internet in marketing yourself.
£10.99   ISBN: 1 902876 81 4

Excel at Interviews
This highly successful book makes invaluable reading for students and jobhunters.
£10.99   ISBN: 1 902876 82 2

Visit us online to view our full range of resources at:
www.lifetime-publishing.co.uk